SCENES FROM THE PAST : 42 (PART ONE)

THE OLDHAM LOO

PART ONE

MANCHES

VICTORIA
TO
SHAW & CROMPTON

VIA HOLLINWOOD, OLDHAM AND ROYTON JUNCTION

The Oldham Loop - 1950s style. Fairburn **42286** brings a Victoria to Rochdale train towards Royton Junction station in July 1957. Ready to leave Royton Junction behind is an Austerity blowing off impatiently at a stop signal near Yates Street bridge. In the foreground stands a row of private owner tank wagons associated with the nearby Higginshaw Gas Works. Tar is a by-product of the pyrolisis of coal and has to be distilled before any practical use can be made of it. The tank wagons were subsequently used to transport the crude tar to a distillery for this process. The nearest rectangular riveted tank (No. 43) is anchored to the chassis by metal straps and further secured by tie-rods between end stanchions. The cylindrical tank is held on timber saddles and is held firmly by both diagonal crossed wire ropes and side tie-rods to the tank ends. The wagons illustrate the quality of freight rolling stock which the post-war railways had inherited.
Jim Davenport

JEFFREY WELLS

Published by Foxline Limited
P O Box 84 Bredbury
Stockport SK6 3YD

In Memory - Jean Wells

This book is published with affectionate memories of my late wife, Jean, whose interest and encouragement kept me running on time.

CONTENTS

Introduction.....................3
Historical summary............5
Reaching Up To Oldham.....6
Miles Platting....................10
Thorpes Bridge................ 12
Dean Lane........................ 13
Failsworth.......................16
Hollinwood.....................19
Impact of Platt Brothers....27
Oldham Werneth..............29

Oldham Central
    and Clegg Street.... 37
Oldham Mumps.................. 52
Royton Junction................79
The Royton Branch...........93
Heyside to Shaw.............101
Shaw & Crompton..............107
Between Shaw
    and Heyside.............114
Shaw in the 1970s & 80s.....120

This book is also dedicated to the memory of Jim Davenport** and Jim Cocker, whose work with a camera will always be revered.

Manchester Victoria, circa 1963. Readers who travelled by train to and from Victoria station in the 1950s and 1960s will no doubt remember these welcoming platform indicators that had served patrons of the Oldham/Rochdale trains for many a year. Decidedly of L&Y origin, these simple but very effective items of platform furniture left nothing to the imagination and could be changed at a moments notice............."*Let our journey around the Oldham Loop commence*".....................................*Authors*

ACKNOWLEDGEMENTS

The writing of and compilation of photographs for 'The Oldham Loop' *(Parts One and Two)* has relied heavily on the generosity of many people who, in one way or another, furnished the 'raw materials'. The list of names is along one and I make no apology if it appears similar to the roll of credits of an epic film. I am indebted to Geoffrey Abbott, Mike Addison, Ron Ames, Jean Bentley, Don Cash, David Carter, Margaret Cocker, Fred Collinge, Bernard Crick, Ray Farrell, Brian Green**, Eric Hall, Arthur Haynes, John Hartshorne, Tom Heavyside, Len Higham, Geoff Hope, Ian Holt, Peter Hutchinson, Jim Peden, Mike Stokes, Roy Welch, Graham Whitehead, and Tom Wray. To specify each person's contribution would be tedious; it is enough to recognise that without their individual assistance and expertise, these books would not exist.

I must also acknowledge the help provided by Greg Fox, who stimulated interest in the project in the first place, and who aided its progress in many ways, particularly with the maps and track diagrams.

I am grateful to Mike Fitton, Photographic Officer of the Lancashire & Yorkshire Railway Society, who kindly gave his consent for me to reproduce many of Eric Blakey's detailed photographs. The local studies sections at the libraries of Middleton, Oldham, Rochdale and Shaw were a rich source of information and I owe much to the personnel who met my requests with patience. My thanks must also go to Martin Smith of the Oldham Evening Chronicle for his help in enabling access to their photographic archives.

Finally, apologies are due to anyone omitted who, in their small way, helped to sort out the wood from the trees.

Jeffrey Wells
Greenfield, Oldham - January 2002

*** The photographs of Jim Davenport appear by courtesy of Brian (B K B) Green.**

THE OLDHAM LOOP
PART ONE

THE GLORY THAT WAS MUMPS STATION, CIRCA 1900. The events leading up to the station as depicted here began in May 1884 when a contract advertisement for a new station appeared in the Manchester Guardian. The contract was let to Thomas Wrigley for £19,508 in June the same year, and by 9 February 1887 the contract was reported to be completed. There were no further developments recorded until May 1913 when a contract for luggage hoists was advertised in the Manchester Guardian. This view was taken from the Down lines; its upward angle shows the magnificent roof sub-structure supported on plain cast iron columns. The columns nearest the camera have a protective wooden cage around the base. Worthy of mention are the pendant gas lights and the ash ballast which is liberally applied over the sleepers. Ash was a cheap commodity in Oldham, derived from the mills which were glad to dispose of it. Beyond the station there are sheeted wagons and a glimpse of an L&Y goods shed. Not missing the opportunity, the station staff pose so as to be included in the photograph. The scene is rich in detail and merits careful study. **Author's Collection**

INTRODUCTION

Within an area of 45 square miles to the north east of Manchester lies the Oldham Loop line, linking the two principal towns - Oldham and Rochdale - and a host of smaller settlements and densely built-up districts close to them. Before 1830 there was but one artery of communication (other than by road) within the area, this being the Rochdale Canal which struck off from the heart of Manchester to breach the Pennine barrier north east of Littleborough. It was the "Rochdale" which formed the blueprint course of the first railway which was to leave "Cottonopolis" (Manchester) and follow closely the line of the Canal as far as Sowerby Bridge in the West Riding of Yorkshire. The Canal and the railway were constant companions, (as they still are) the latter outliving the former as a major transport route.

The other lines which finally formed the Loop arrived on the scene in stages much later but the whole was completed by 1880 so that it was possible by then to set off from Manchester

Victoria station, pass through Oldham and Rochdale, and return to the starting point. The journey could be done in reverse, of course.

Even before the Loop was completed, however, several other lines had left or joined the parent line between Manchester and Littleborough. Two of these impinged on the principal towns: the renowned Oldham Branch with its severe gradient up to the western periphery of Oldham, and the Bacup Branch which left Rochdale on a tight curve leading away from the main line.

The Loop line stimulated industrial growth and population movement. A number of Nineteenth Century industrial concerns which found themselves close to the Loop, or had deliberately chosen a location near to it, took advantage of large private sidings. In Oldham, Platt Bros. Ltd. had sidings in two locations; at Castleton, Tweedale & Smalley; Oldham Corporation had its Higginshaw Gas Works leading off the Royton Branch; whilst at Shaw, Platt Bros.' Jubilee Colliery Sidings on the approach to

New Hey were in full use. Even during the present century, sidings were laid in several locations to serve a variety of concerns. Ferranti Sidings at Hollinwood, and the CEGB sidings at Chadderton are but two examples.

There can be few people who have not travelled on the Loop line to work, for shopping and entertainment. Perhaps fewer can now recall their annual excursion to Blackpool or North Wales which started at New Hey or Royton, Moston or Middleton, Rochdale or Shaw. I for one have memories of catching an overnight train from Hollinwood station, along with other bleary-eyed families, all destined for the balmy clime of Tor Bay, when the Devon Riviera was a popular as Ibiza and the Costa Brava are today. In the 1950s the journey to Torquay or Ilfracombe was an exotic journey from one world to another.

Although under threat of closure on more than one occasion the Loop line has survived almost intact albeit with modifications. Dr Beeching outlined the problem of suburban lines (The Re-Shaping of British Railways, 1963): *"In the passenger field, stopping trains are by far the worst loss maker. These trains, which derive little advantage from the speed of rail movement, are known to be very lightly loaded and to run, very largely, on routes which carry little traffic of any kind"*. Perhaps it was comments such as this that prompted BR to close the Manchester - Oldham - Rochdale line (the eastern portion of the Loop line) in 1964. It was certainly recommended by the Doctor

in Section 2 of his document (Passenger Services to be Modified). (Section 1 actually recommended the withdrawal of services between Manchester Victoria - Newton Heath and Middleton) The Manchester Victoria - Oldham - Rochdale line was reprieved but services were reduced and stations were closed: Oldham Central was one of Oldham's three main stations which closed on 18 April 1966. In 1971 it looked as though the line between Oldham and Rochdale was to close, but again this was not carried out, although the section of line between Shaw and Rochdale was singled in 1980.

History books published in (say) 2025 will have the benefit of the next 25 years to analyse events. By then, the electrified Metrolink route between Manchester and Rochdale via Oldham will be old hat. Proponents of the abandoned LYR third rail electrification scheme of 1916, linking Manchester and Rochdale by almost the same route will peer down from the great railway platform in the sky and be justifiably proud to be able to say *"We thought of it first"*.

Fortunately for us the Loop line was well-photographed by interested parties in the 1950s and 1960s. Such images from the basis for this book - the Loop line as it used to be captured on photographic film by a band of enthusiastic cameramen. An outline of the chronological history of the Loop line is worth recording for it will not forever be with us - at least not in its present form. This is how the book begins.

A classic view of Royton Junction in the late 1950s would have been like this, with the focus of attention claimed by Fairburn **42283** setting off with a Rochdale to Victoria train, next stop, Oldham Mumps. Meanwhile, impatiently blowing off in the yard, is a 'Austerity' 8F waiting for a road with a rake of open wagons. The yard was quite extensive and had a wagon capacity of 414. On this occasion the yard is crowded with open wagons, sheeted-up loads, and at least one van.

Jim Davenport

Rochdale train at platform 7, Stanier 2-6-4T **42475** (26D, Bury shed) awaits departure with the 5.15pm Rochdale service from Victoria's platform 7, 22 April 1951. An unidentified tank engine stands alongside still bearing LMS livery despite a lapse of three years since Nationalisation. Spanning the bay platforms is the wrought iron lattice luggage bridge which, by means of electric lifts, (originally hydraulic) luggage trolleys could be conveyed from platform to platform, from one side of the station to the other. The bridge was erected over the bay platforms in 1904 when the station was enlarged. It was partially demolished sometime in 1949 but a substantial section survived for another four decades. *H C Casserley*

MANCHESTER to LITTLEBOROUGH - *A PIONEERING VENTURE*

The Manchester & Leeds Railway Company's line opened as far as Littleborough (actually a few yards short of the Summit Tunnel) on 3 July 1839. For practical purposes the sixteen miles length of line stretched from the Manchester terminus at Oldham Road to a temporary station at Littleborough. The first travellers on opening day were conveyed in two trains, the first starting its journey at 12.22pm, the second ten minutes later. At 1.29 the first train arrived at Rochdale station, *where the concourse of people was very great, and the cheering crowds on and around the line, aided by bands of music, showed the cordial greeting with which the people of Rochdale were disposed to welcome so beneficial a communication with the great centre and capital of the cotton manufacture. (The Railway Times, 13 July 1839).* Rochdale station house was described as being quite finished, except for the interior fittings. The station roof was bedecked with "a number of flags" as were other buildings close to the line. The "beneficial communication" had taken almost two years to reach fruition since work first began on 18 August 1837 in two places: at Newton Heath, and at Royle Farm, Castleton.

The early timetable (dated 27 July 1839) showed there to be four stations between Manchester and the Summit Tunnel: Mills Hill (which served Oldham and surrounding areas), Blue Pits (Castleton), Rochdale, and Littleborough. Trains left

Manchester on the hour on the first day of public service at 8am, the last at 7pm, with noticeable gaps at midday, 2pm and 5pm. The journey to was timed at 45 minutes for which a well-to-do person would pay 3 shillings First Class, and a stand-up Third Class traveller 1 shilling. There were no trains on Sundays, (in deference to the Sabbatarian movement) and it was forbidden to pay gratuities to the Company's servants, or to smoke.

At Blue Pits, a single line branching west to Heywood was opened on 15 April 1841. This had the distinction of not having been authorised by Parliament, and to have been horse-drawn from the beginning. It was not until an M&L Act of 30 June 1845 that there was an intention to double the line, and not until 1 May 1848 that the line had been doubled. The Manchester Guardian, 5 May 1847, found space to announce that *On Saturday passenger trains from Heywood to Blue Pits were propelled by locomotive engines for the first time, having been previously drawn by horses.*

The town of Oldham was a difficult one to reach by railway owing to its elevated position in the western foothills of the Pennines. As early as June 1839 discussion about a rail link to the town was in progress because it was felt *"That the present means of communication by land between Manchester and Oldham is insufficient for agricultural, commercial, manufacturing, and other purposes; and there is no communication by water".* (The

Railway Times, 1 June 1839). *It was recognised that reaching Oldham by rail was not easy:".... there is an inclined plane with an inclination of 1 in 30 for a distance of 2,580 yards, and an inclination on 1 in 132 for a distance of 138 yards, which it is proposed should be worked by a stationery engine".* (Ibid). Thus from an engineering point of view a branch to Oldham was not favourable; it was considered, however, to be the best "the country will afford". The route which had been decided upon, from a junction near Middleton to the dizzy heights of Werneth had to take cognisance of the fact that *"The town of Oldham cannot be approached by railway, except by incline planes, or very circuitous routes and very hard curves". (Ibid).*

Undaunted, the M&L constructed its so-called Oldham Branch which was completed and inspected by Lt. Colonel Pasley of the Board of Trade on 24 March 1842. The Manchester Guardian noted that the works had been of "somewhat arduous character" but that the difficulties had been surmounted. The Branch was opened for public use on 31 March 1842, the junction with the main line being at "Oldham Junction", and the terminus at a tunnel entrance a few yards east of Werneth station. This was to be Oldham's only station for the next five years.

When the line between Manchester and Normanton had been completed on 1 March 1841 trains stopped at Rochdale en route to Leeds by way of Normanton, or were on the final leg of their journey in the opposite direction. Rochdale became an important railway focus, possessing a station, goods facilities, an engine shed, plus the status of a reserved water station, meaning that locomotives could take water there, but only when necessary.

The Oldham terminus in Manchester was short-lived. On 1 January 1844 the M&L proudly opened its new station at Hunt's Bank, proclaiming it to be known as the Victoria Station. From this date, all trains to Rochdale and beyond left Victoria and climbed the steep incline (1 in 59) out of the station on a viaduct, then at 1 in 47 over streets and roof tops before reaching Miles Platting station. This was achieved at first by rope haulage and soon after without the aid of a stationary engine at the head of the incline. Oldham Road station became a goods only terminus from 1 January the same year.

The improved timetable for 1841 showed that there were eight trains in both directions between Manchester and Leeds with a reduced service both ways on Sundays. By 1841, Sabbatarianism was being challenged by many Companies except in stricter Scotland. A typical train was the 7 am from Victoria station which called at every station, taking three hours to reach Leeds. In the return direction, a faster train was the 4 pm from Leeds which stopped at fewer stations (including Rochdale), taking 2 hours 45 minutes to reach Manchester.

On the 9 July 1847 the pioneering M&L changed its name to the Lancashire & Yorkshire Railway - the same company with a different name and with wide ambitions. For the next 76 years this Company's trains traversed the line between Manchester and Rochdale: through expresses, local passenger trains, luggage and goods trains, and excursion trains. It was during the LYR reign that two further branch lines were constructed even though each had their origins in M&L days. The first to be opened was the Middleton Branch on 5 January 1857. The line left Middleton Junction (formerly Oldham Junction) on a tight curve and bore westwards on a falling gradient for 1 mile 6 chains to the terminus at Middleton.

The second branch line left the main line just north of Rochdale station, and like the Middleton Branch, left the town on a tight curve of 18 chains radius, on a sinuous course to reach the Rossendale town of Bacup. The Branch was opened for passenger traffic after protracted delays and construction difficulties on 1 November 1870. An official announcement appeared in the Manchester Guardian on the day of opening. Readers read that *"Opening of the Shawforth Branch. The public are respectively informed that on and after Tuesday, November 1 1870, the above branch will be opened for passenger traffic".* The first station out of Rochdale was Wardleworth, a little over one mile from Rochdale station.

In creating the line between Manchester and Rochdale the M&L company unwittingly formed the western leg of the Oldham Loop line. And just as Rochdale had become an important stopping and watering place, so Oldham to the east was to become the next focus of attention involving an interplay between three railway companies, namely, the Lancashire & Yorkshire Railway, the London and North Western Railway, and the Manchester, Sheffield & Lincolnshire Railway.

REACHING UP TO OLDHAM

The first line to head for Oldham had to negotiate the steep ascent from Oldham Junction (re-named Middleton Junction in August 1852). The line left the junction on a tight curve, crossed the Rochdale Canal, and progressed eastwards towards Werneth where Oldham's first station was situated. Oldham Junction lay 343ft above sea level; Werneth, $1\frac{3}{4}$ miles to the east, stood at 525ft. The average upward gradient was 1 in $53\frac{1}{2}$ but this disguises a 1 in 27 incline on the approach to the terminus. The latter was an inconveniently located amenity just over a mile from the town centre. In this respect Werneth station was not so much different to Rochdale station which lay just under a mile from the heart of Rochdale. On the other hand, Werneth station was conveniently close to the Manchester to Oldham turnpike road, and to Featherstall Road South (connecting Oldham and Royton). Werneth station, despite its eccentric location was a far better proposition for the local people than a two mile traipse by road to Mills Hill station.

With abandonment of rope haulage, reliance was placed upon locomotive power alone to ascend the incline. The first engine to accomplish this under its own steam was engine No. 131, a Jenkins "Bury" 2-2-2 single. John Marshall *(The Lancashire & Yorkshire Railway, Vol.3, 62)* mentions a second engine accomplishing the same feat. *"Another, number 151, driven by William Hurst, took the first regular train of six carriages up to Oldham without the rope in 1851".* William Hurst was the LYR's outdoor superintendent.

In 1855 William Jenkins (the LYR locomotive engineer) designed the 0-6-0 "Oldham Incline Engines". As the name

All trains leaving Victoria for Oldham and Rochdale passed Turntable signal box. This excellent view shows the box on 22 June 1960, along with adjacent parachute water column, ballast box, and electric yard lamp. Turntable box (LY 235) was opened in 1903/4 and located 112 yards from the bay platforms. Housing 124 levers it controlled points and signals for the local trains. It was closed on 7 April 1962. In the background are the gas holders of the Corporation's Rochdale Road Gas Works, and the Co-operative Insurance building which displayed the words Complete Insurance Services. It was from one of the rear windows that Jim Roberts (a contributor to this book) discovered that from his desk he had an unrestricted view of Victoria East Junction - certainly a bonus for a new recruit in the employ of the Co-op. The building now constitutes the Parkers Hotel, 109, Corporation Street. *Graham Whitehead*

implies, these passenger saddle tanks were designed for this particular route. LYR Board Minutes of 1 September 1857 refer to a "new train" running between Manchester and Oldham consisting *"of three carriages weighing 8 tons each, carrying 204 passengers. Its length is 108 feet. It is equal to the 8 carriages of the old set, which would weigh 5 tons each."*

Plans to extend the line one mile further east were prepared by Thomas Gooch in 1844. The extension was to be a single line which was forced to pass through two tunnels before reaching the new terminus at Mumps. In the event, a double line was laid through the Werneth Tunnel (471 yards) and the Central Tunnel (449 yards), these being separated by a 200 yards long deep cutting. The tunnels were necessary in order to penetrate an elevated ridge of high ground upon which the central part of Oldham is situated. An intermediate station was established beyond the eastern end of the Central Tunnel and this was recognised by the Manchester Guardian, 23 October 1847, before its opening. *"The Town Station will be of a temporary character, but it is to be fully improved as soon as the time will allow. It is situate at the bottom of Clegg Street, now in the course of formation;*

and, until the road is completed, the road to the station will be alongside the front of the gasworks and through Greaves Street". Central station was indeed more central to the town than either Werneth or Mumps stations. The Town Station opened, along with Mumps, on 1 November 1847, the day on which the one mile extension opened to passenger traffic.

Despite the convenience of Central station it was Mumps at the eastern periphery of the town which became the most significant station. A map of 1848 shows that the station building stood in grand isolation, apparently surrounded by open land and close by Mumps Mill, a textile mill. One platform served the station alongside which a single line ran and terminated a short distance beyond. An engine release line allowed engines to run round their trains and rejoin the single line at the other end for the return journey.

The LYR, having reached Oldham as far as Werneth, it was probably inevitable that the LNWR should take up the previously projected line of its predecessor (the Huddersfield & Manchester Company) to reach the town. As early as 1845 the formation of a line to run from a junction at Greenfield in

Saddleworth to Oldham had been discussed. Several years elapsed, however, before a final survey was completed in July 1852 by the eminent engineer Joseph Locke.

Following trials runs on 12 April and 1 May 1856 the completed line was opened to the public on Friday, 4 July with due celebration. The Oldham Chronicle the day after was full of approbation: *"The line is a very well-constructed one and as smooth and level as could be desired; forming in this respect a marked contrast with some others in the neighbourhood, under the able management of C Cooper Esq. the Superintendent of this division of the lines of the London and North Western Company to whose activity and kind attention the passengers were much indebted for the excellent arrangements"*. The LNWR's Victoria station at Mumps was a separate entity, and had no physical connection with the LYR's station close by. An OS map of 1865 shows the abandoned station situated north of the LNWR's running lines. By this date the opening of Glodwick Road station and the OAGB's Clegg Street station had usurped the old Victoria station. Facing the old station building was a single-line engine shed and a nearby coal depot. To complete the LNWR's complement of facilities there was a weighing machine, yard crane, water column, "signalman's box", and a locomotive turntable. A connection between the two companies' lines lay to the west of the two stations. People had the opportunity of using Glodwick Road station on and after 1 November 1862. The Oldham Chronicle on the same day grudgingly acknowledged the fact with the terse statement that *"The new station at Glodwick Road will be opened today"*. No fuss - no ceremony.

Early services between Greenfield and Oldham were generous with nine trains each way, Monday to Saturday. Two Parliamentary trains ran each day in both directions, the first train leaving at an unearthly early hour from each place. On Sundays, four trains ran each way, two of these being Parliamentary trains on which those passengers of lowly means had to pay 1d per mile.

The real benefit of the LNWR line lay in the services from the small village of Delph. Passing through such stations as Grasscroft Halt, Grotton, Lees, and Glodwick Road, the line served the communities east of Oldham with regular passenger trains from the Saddleworth area with connections to Manchester and Stockport, and gave Oldhamers the chance to connect with Yorkshire-bound trains from Manchester via Ashton and Stalybridge. In LMS days Delph had the description *"village and railway terminus, LMS, W.R.Yorks, 6 miles N.E. of Ashton-under-Lyne"* in one gazetteer of the British Iles. Regular services between Oldham Clegg Street station and Delph finally ceased running on 30 April 1955, the official closure of the line falling on 2 May.

The Oldham, Ashton & Guide Bridge Junction Railway was authorised by Act of Parliament, 10 August 1857. The original scheme had five elements, only one of which had a direct impact on Oldham. This was the line starting from a junction at Ashton with the LYR, west of Charlestown station (Ashton East Junction) to Clegg Street station, a distance of 3½ miles. When completed in 1861 the line was jointly operated by the LNWR and the MS&LR, Oldham being approached on its southern flanks - a much easier proposition than the approach from the west. According to Neil Fraser (The Railway Observer, June 1963), *"It had been intended to have the station at Oldham located at Rhodes Bank, alongside and between the LYR Central and Mumps stations, but this was opposed by the latter and so the site at Clegg Street was chosen"*. The first train to traverse the line from Guide Bridge ran over the metals on 1 June 1861, this consisting of an engine and two carriages. The official opening took place on 31 July when a decorated engine and thirty carriages set off from London Road station, Manchester, carrying no less a personage that Charles Sacre, the MS&LR's locomotive superintendent, riding on the footplate.

Although Ashton would benefit from the new railway, it was considered that Oldham was the main beneficiary. A report on the opening run maintained that *"Oldham will be the greater gainer, as it opens out to that town direct communication with the east and south of England, and gives it ready access to the valuable coalfields near this town"*. (Stalybridge Reporter, 3 August 1861). Apart from the rejoicing crowds which lined the route, the opening day was attended by directors and officials of both the LNWR and MS&LR. Noticeably absent was any representation by the LYR which felt peeved ....***continued on page 12***

The photographer caught a scene of ageing infrastructure and optimistic renewal when he pointed his camera towards Victoria East Junction signal box on 22 June 1960. The inveterate box opened its doors as LY 196 in 1899 and accommodated 108 levers (99w 9s) to keep a team of bobbies occupied until 1947 when the number of levers was reduced to 96. Closure took place on 7 April 1962. Behind the old box, the shape of things to come. The steel-framed replacement power box had yet to be completed and was opened on 2 April in the same year. With the closure of Victoria East Junction, Turntable, Millgate, Newtown 1 and 2, and Footbridge signal boxes the new box took control over signalling as far as Cheetham Hill Junction and Collyhurst Street. Section C notices at this time indicate that the running signals were removed and replaced by multi-aspect colour signalling with continuous track circuiting, all controlled from the new power box. The work was undertaken during the weekend of Friday, 30 March to Monday, 2 April 1962. The removal of the old boxes and the semaphore signalling took away the L&Y heritage on the eastern approaches to the station. *Graham Whitehead*

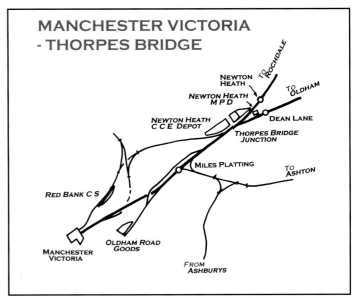

(Left) Drivers of DMUs travelling out of Victoria on the Down Slow line had this view of Millgate signal box through their cab window. Situated 264 yards from East Junction box, LY 234 opened in 1904 with an L&Y 78 lever frame positioned on the west side of the box, directly above the brick base. The restricted space at this location forced the Company to erect a box with a narrow base with the operating floor overhanging on the east side. The photograph was taken on 2 September 1959 by Graham Whitehead who has taken advantage of an invitation to ride in the cab on a journey northwards. Millgate box closed on 7 April 1962. *Graham Whitehead*

MANCHESTER VICTORIA - THORPES BRIDGE

Almost at the top of Hunt's Bank Incline, 1 mile 44$\frac{1}{2}$ chains from Victoria station, stood girder bridge number 13 which conveyed two lines from New Allen Street Junction (on the Oldham Road Goods Branch) over the main line. In the upper photograph, the four tracks constituted (from left to right) Down Fast; Up Fast; Down Slow; and Up Slow. The gradient at this location was 1 in 49. Bridge No.13 was erected about 1890 as part of the widening of the Oldham Road Branch, the Hunt's Bank Incline up to Miles Platting, and the Ashton Branch as far as Baguley Fold. Reference to the bridge appeared in the Manchester Guardian, 30 May 1889, when it was reported that *A new double line will be constructed from the Oldham Road branch and will be carried over the main passenger lines at a point a short distance on the Manchester side of Collyhurst Street, by a girder bridge of 42ft span. It was demolished in June 1978.* *British Railways*

(Left) On 2 September 1959, the photographer took advantage of the forward view then available to passengers from the front of the DMU as it approaches Miles Platting Junction. The low retaining wall on the left marks the elevated approach to bridge No. 13 - now behind us - which carried the lines to and from Brewery Sidings. A train hauled by a 'Black Five' begins the descent to Victoria station on an adjacent 'road'.
Graham Whitehead

MILES PLATTING 'BANK'

(Below) Working hard, un-rebuilt 'Royal Scot' Class, 7P **46158** *The Loyal Regiment,* draws its train up the Hunt's Bank Incline, and is probably working a Liverpool Exchange to York or Newcastle service sometime in the early 1950s. A fine lattice gantry supported an assemblage of signals for control of the Down direction at this location, to the west of Miles Platting station.
Arthur Bendell

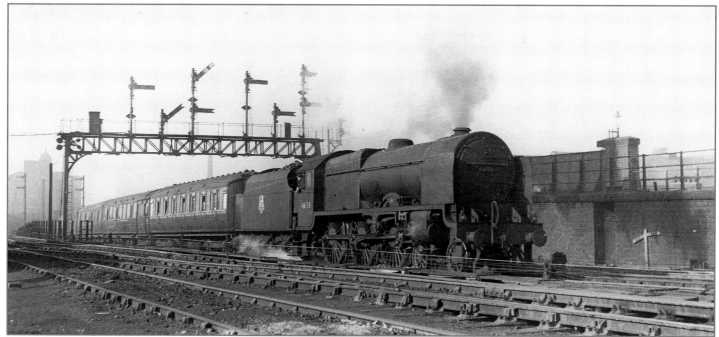

This 1956 view from the direction of Collyhurst Street signal box shows to the left the Goods lines serving Oldham Roads Goods. It also serves to illustrate the rapidity with which the 'main' line falls away down Hunts Bank Incline, 1 in 47 at this point. The intersection bridge to the right carries the goods lines between Oldham Road and Tank Yard/Brewery Sidings, avioding any conflict with th main lines. Tank Yard had a capacity for 515 wagons, whilst Brewery could hold 920. The provision of sight boards behind the signal arms was essential due to the dark background caused by buildings and other structures, particlarly the bridge.
C H A Townley, courtesy J Peden

MILES PLATTING

(Above) A very early reference to Miles Platting station appeared in the Manchester Guardian, 23 December 1843, in which it was stated that *a passenger station is also to be opened at the Miles Platting Junction, for the convenience of parties living in the neighbourhood of Failsworth, Hollingwood [sic] and Newton Heath…..* The station seems to have been opened on 1 January 1844. On 17 January 1846 reference to further developments at the station was made in the same newspaper: to the whole of the works required in the erection of the Miles Platting station on the Ashton Branch. The station as it appears in this photograph owes its disposition to the rebuilding which took place in 1890 coincident with the widening scheme. Board of Trade sanction for the widening scheme was given on 15 June 1892. The view is towards Rochdale and the down platform, photographed on 1 June 1968. The low brick and glazed structure constituted a covered passage leading from a subway beneath the running lines from the entrance on Lamb Lane. A similar structure existed on the up side, the end of which stands behind the speed limit sign. *J P Alsop*

(Centre) Aspinall 'A' Class 0-6-0 goes about its business in the Miles Platting area. *R Keeley*

BREWERY SIDINGS

(Right-lower) The western aspect of Brewery Sidings signal box caught on camera, 18 September 1976. Opening as LY 229 on 21 April 1894, Brewery Sidings was located on the up side, south of Monsall Lane bridge. It replaced an earlier box of 1890 which had also been located south of the bridge, but on the down side. This early box had been closed owing to the widening of the railway between 1889 and 1891. The second box housed an L&Y 54 lever frame, finally extended to 64 when the new curve to the Ashton Branch was laid in 1906. Like its neighbour, Brewery Sidings fell victim of modernisation in the summer of 1998. *J A Sommerfield*

continued from page 8............by the OAGB line into Oldham, perceiving it to be, no doubt, a direct threat of competition.

The people of Oldham owed a great deal to one of its elders Edmund Buckley who had also been instrumental in the Mumps to Greenfield line. The OAGB line was seen as vitally important to the town because *"By the new line they should have 13 trains to and from Manchester, seven from Oldham to Liverpool, and five from Liverpool to Oldham; ten from Oldham to London; five by the Great Northern and five by the London and North Western; and eight trains from London to Oldham". (Ibid).*

Turning to Neil Fraser again, we learn that *"The portion of the line beyond Clegg Street was not complete while at Mumps a new warehouse was being built, and earth moved from here was taken a short distance and used to widen the line alongside the L&Y line, a single line being laid for the purpose". (Ibid).*

One section of the eastern leg of the Oldham Loop had yet to be constructed between Mumps station and Rochdale. Dissatisfaction with the Oldham Branch in the 1840s led to the promotion of two rival schemes which would provide a direct link between Manchester and Oldham. These two schemes failed to materialise but with the support of the M&L a new bill was placed before Parliament entitled *"Oldham Alliance Railway Company"*.

The bill received Royal Assent on 22 July 1847. One of its aims was to link Mumps with Rochdale, along with a branch line to Royton.

In 1847 the Oldham Alliance scheme was carried forward by the M&L, but owing to a shortage of capital it was abandoned in 1850. It was revived nine years later, the Oldham to Rochdale element appearing as the LYR's *"Rochdale & Royton Branches Act"*. Work began on the line in 1862 with contracts for stations at Royton, Royton Junction, Shaw, New Hey, and Milnrow. James Gow was the contractor for the construction of the line, and Patrick Farrell the contractor for the stations.

The 6 miles 54 chain line was opened for goods traffic on 12 August 1863; the Royton Branch on 12 March 1864. Passenger traffic commenced running between the two towns on 2 November 1863, and along the short (less than a mile) branch to Royton on 21 March 1864. The public opening of the Oldham - Rochdale line was acknowledged in the Oldham Chronicle a few days later, 7 November. *"On Monday, trains commenced running from Oldham to Rochdale on the new line via Shaw. On the Saturday before, a train conveyed a number of directors, including George Wilson Esq., (the Chairman) along the line. Since the opening of the railway, a goodly number of passengers has been conveyed along the line, and the inhabitants of Shaw and that dis-*

THORPES BRIDGE

Depending upon the direction of travel, this was the location where the Oldham Loop line began or ended, at a distance of 2¹/₄ miles from Victoria. This important junction lay under the control of Thorpes Bridge Junction signal box. The first box opened in 1877 in preparation for the opening of the Manchester Loop line and the Hollinwood Branch and was positioned on the up side at the junction. This earlier box was closed in 1899 and replaced by L&Y 191, measuring 62ft x 12ft. Changes came in 1943 when the box received an LMS 135 lever frame, facing east towards the camera. During the changeover two frames existed in the box, but only one, of course, was in use during this time. Closure came on 26 September 1987. Of equal interest are the changes to Thorpes Bridge. The original M&L bridge was a 26ft span brick arch over two lines. Before the Manchester Loop line and the Hollinwood Branch were opened (1878 and 1880 respectively) the arch was demolished and a new bridge built using wrought iron girders and floor-plates. Four lines passed beneath the 61ft span with an adjoining single line span (14ft 6ins) serving internal works traffic. The bridge was extended on the eastern side in 1898 to span the Hollinwood Branch which was realigned. In 1970 the 61ft span was reconstructed using pre-cast concrete beams and brick parapets. The left span was designated Bridge No.1 on the Hollinwood Branch; the wide span becoming Bridge No.19 on the main line to Rochdale, and 16 on the Manchester Loop line. Date of photograph: 10 February 1974. *J A Sommerfield*

DEAN LANE

The outlook across the tracks from Dean Lane signal box was far from interesting, facing as it did a brick retaining wall. Behind the box, lined up and awaiting their fate, are three ex-L&Y 0-6-0s: from front to back these include **52558, 52207**, and **52358**. The line-up was photographed on 22 April 1951, the forlorn trio caught in the lens over a mountain of coal in the stacking area. The small signal box opened as LY 228 in 1880 and was a product of the Gloucester Wagon Company which, despite its name, was a signalling contractor. With only 15 levers to operate by the 1890s it was an easy box to work. Its levers were pulled for the last time on 28 June 1957, on the day of closure.   *H C Casserley*

trict have made an extensive use of the improved method of communication with Oldham". The arrangements for passengers travelling to Shaw or Rochdale from Manchester necessitated a change of trains at Mumps station. Likewise, passengers changed trains on the return journey. This suggests that there were no through trains between Manchester and Rochdale, a temporary expedient according to the newspaper report. Four Third Class trains ran each weekday and on Sundays from Oldham to Rochdale; three in the other direction. With characteristic parochial charm the Chronicle's report ended by noting that *"The inhabitants of Shaw and its vicinity are respectfully informed that they can get their hair cut or dressed on Saturday at Jones' Hairdressing Rooms, 32, Manchester Street, Oldham, opposite Mr Joseph Rug's Tinplate Works".*

The opening of the Royton Branch received similar treatment by the Oldham Chronicle on 26 March 1864: *"On Monday morning the first passenger train arrived at the Royton station at 8.15 and was greeted by hundreds of the inhabitants. Sixty eight passengers proceeded to Oldham and other parts on its return. They arrived at the Mumps station in seven minutes. During the day 198 tickets were sold at the Royton station, and 105 came in. Upon several of the mills and other places, colours were flying in*

honour of the event. In the evening a public dinner was held at the Railway Inn".

Royton Wakes were given coverage by the same newspaper in August 1864. Evidently the railway was a great boon to the district in conveying people to and from their favourite haunts: *"The public houses were well-patronised during the evening and towards nine o'clock the railway station became inconveniently crowded by several hundred persons anxious to make their way home, and although additional carriages were attached to the ordinary train, the accommodation was not sufficient for all and an extra train had to be provided later in the evening".*

The meagre services operating when the Oldham to Rochdale line first opened were quickly improved upon and settled down to the following format:

Oldham to Rochdale, Monday to Saturday
6.05   8.05   10.15   11.30   12.55pm   2.00   4.20   5.27   6.26   8.20
Rochdale to Oldham, Monday to Saturday
8.45   11.00   12.10pm   1.25   3.20   4.50   5.45   7.00   9.00
Sundays
9.40   1.30pm
5.10   9.00 from each station.

Note that there were no through trains at this stage.
Source: Oldham Chronicle, November 1963.

....*continued on page 15*

A small group of people (porter and workmen) steps forward to meet the arrival of the 12.05 train to Royton on 12 April 1957. Unlike Failsworth and Hollinwood stations, Dean Lane had a ceramic non-slip platform surface and an rail edge of flags. The veteran brick platform buildings were pure L&Y. The Manchester Courier briefly mentioned the station on 17 May 1880, on the opening of the Hollinwood Branch: *Here the booking office is on a higher level and the platforms, 200 yards long, are connected by an iron, covered footbridge. Messrs E Taylor, of Littleborough, was the contractor.* Another feature of the station was its position in a shallow cutting, unlike its neighbours which were perched on an embankment. The station is still open, now shorn of its brick buildings and footbridge.

H C Casserley

Dean Lane station, looking west, on 11 October 1959. Two human figures shuffle towards the up platform from beneath Dean Lane bridge (No 2 on the Hollinwood Branch). This was the unofficial way taken by scores of railwaymen passing between Newton Heath shed and the station. A substantial covered and half-glazed footbridge connected the platforms, the up side end joining the station booking office the entrance to which faced Dean Lane. In 1959 the first station out of Victoria on the Branch was manned, a situation marked by the tidy and litter-free platforms. My paternal grandfather preferred to use this station for his daily trip into Manchester during the 1920s, in preference to Newton Heath station which was nearer to his home.

H C Casserley

(Left) The Hollinwood Branch was not usually associated with heavy freight traffic but in the mid-1960s, following discussions with Rochdale UDC regarding smoke pollution, more freight trains found their way on to the severely-graded route to Oldham. The heaviest of these required banking assistance and in late 1967 an example of one such was photographed at Dean Lane station. The train had probably started its journey at Brewery Sidings and is destined for Royton Junction Sidings, hauled by a 8F 48373. The next three miles would provide a stern test, with gradients as steep as 1 in 52/44 on the approach to Werneth. The number of the banker is not known.

Paul Jordan, courtesy Bernard Crick

On 25 June 1966, Eric Blakey found himself at Dean Lane station. Eric made it his personal mission during the 1960s to photograph as many ex-L&Y structures as possible before they succumbed to the thrust of modern-isation. In the photograph, at platform level, we can see that Eric was too late to include the booking office which had been removed, leaving the up platform stairs and footbridge isolated from each other. The sloping brick retaining wall facing Dean Lane signal box is visible through Dean Lane bridge. The second photograph was taken through absent glazing in the footbridge. It shows the eastern approach to the station, framed by the ironwork of a right-hand bracket signal. This end of the Branch is frequently crossed by bridges; the one in the distance (Bridge No.4) carried Reliance Street.
LYRS Collection

Continued from page 13.......

One element of the Oldham Alliance Railway proposal had been that of a direct link between Manchester and Oldham. The line between Miles Platting (Thorpes Bridge Junction) and Werneth had to wait until it was taken on board by Sturges Meek, the LYR engineer, on 3 November 1858. An estimate of £250,000 was given as the cost of construction of such a rail link. Seventeen years were to elapse before definite plans were drawn up for this overdue and very much needed line, the delay in any progress probably can be attributed to escalating construction costs. On 1 May 1875 the Manchester Guardian had space for an LYR contract advertisement which announced that the Directors were prepared to receive tenders *"for the construction of a Branch Railway being about 4 miles in length"*. On the following 30 June James Evans was awarded the contract for a sum of £104,000. Works seems to have commenced as and when land became available, at the close of 1875 and the beginning of 1876.

The completed line was inspected by General C S Hutchinson CE at the start of May 1880. The opening day occurred on 17 May, a fact which was noted by the Manchester Courier on the same day, by giving a description of the new line. *"The line, which is about 4 miles long and generally follows the turnpike road between Manchester and Oldham, joins at Werneth, the main line from Middleton Junction to Oldham. It avoids the heavy gradient of 1 in 27 between these two places, the ruling gradient of the new line being 1 in 50. In future, the whole of the*

Manchester to Oldham traffic will be carried via Hollinwood, the distance being about half a mile less that way". The Oldham Chronicle of one day in June 1880 provided a comprehensive coverage of train services to and from Oldham. The following is an outline of the number of trains which stopped at Hollinwood station, the principal intermediate station on the new route:

Oldham to Manchester (weekdays)
30 trains: earliest - 5.20am; latest - 10.40pm.
Manchester to Oldham (weekdays)
30 trains: earliest - 5.20am; latest - 11.31pm.
Oldham to Manchester (Sundays)
9 trains: earliest -7.30 am; latest - 10.10 pm.
Manchester to Oldham (Sundays)
9 trains: earliest - 9.29 am; latest - 11.05 pm.

By May 1880 the Oldham Loop line was fully completed, not that it was referred by this name until well into the present century. Unlike Rochdale which stood on a major cross-Pennine inter-city route, Oldham never saw main line trains services. Instead, it was a nodal point of three distinct railway routes which were operated by three independent companies, namely, Manchester Victoria, via Oldham to Rochdale, either through Hollinwood or Middleton Junction - LYR; Greenfield Junction to Oldham - LNWR; Ashton to Oldham - OAGB. Despite handling local traffic only, the town could boast that it possessed five stations, putting the town on a par with nearby Manchester.

DEAN LANE

(Right-lower) Taking advantage of the absence of glazing in the footbridge, Eric has captured the eastern approach to Dean Lane station, looking towards Failsworth. The bridge in the distance is No. 4 carrying Reliance Street over the line. This section of line is frequently crossed by bridges, there being ten between Dean Lane and Failsworth stations. The iron rail forms the handrail of the right-hand bracket signal seen in the previous photograph.
Eric Blakey, LYRS Collection

Hardman Lane, Failsworth, 21 January 1910. An Edwardian view of the township's amenity on a miserable wet day. The L&Y embellished the prosaic station entrance by erecting a gas lamp on a wrought iron bracket. The corbelled roof line was a further concession to ornament as was the use of yellow brickwork to lighten the building. Close by, two advertisements inform passers-by: one claims the benefits of Wagstaff's Pianos which could be bought at 15 Mary's Gate, Piccadilly, and 260 Ashton Old Road, Manchester. The other extols the pleasures of smoking BDV tobacco. The large notice on the opposite side advertises the Colliseum Theatre Oldham, The Grand Pantomime "Hop o' my Thumb", Matinees every Tuesday and Saturday. On the embankment is a timber signal post with a lower-quadrant co-acting arm in the off position. ***Technical Services Dept. Manchester City Council***

FAILSWORTH

Hardman Lane and the entrance to Failsworth station on 25 June 1966. The Branch at this location is carried on an embankment, with the gradient rising towards Oldham at 1 in 55. To reach the platforms it was necessary to enter the doorway of the booking office, then ascend one or other set of stairs; the down side could be reached by way of a subway. The painted message on the bridge parapet left no doubt as to where the station entrance was - a boon to people with poor eyesight looking for the station from a distance. ***Eric Blakey LYRS Collection***

Failsworth station was the last station to be constructed on the Branch, the Oldham Daily Standard, 2 April 1881, announcing that on the day before…. *the Failsworth Railway station was opened for traffic.* It was described as handsome and commodious, and it was anticipated that it would be well-used. In contrast to Dean Lane, the L&Y made much use of timber, along with brick walls and stone dressings. Both platforms were supported on a substantial timber framework bedded into the sides of the embankment. Eric Blakey visited the station with friend and colleague John Hodgson who is leaning in a casual manner against an up platform building. The view is towards Manchester on what appears to be a dull summer day.

Eric Blakey LYRS Collection

(Left) **In the Station Master's office at Failsworth station**, Eric Blakey focused on this double-seated slatted bench, a one-time piece of high comfort furniture courtesy of the L&Y. The photograph was taken on 25 June 1966 suggesting that the bench had been in service for 60 years or more. The crumbling brickwork indicates that the fabric of the building has fared less well over the years.

LYRS Collection

(Below) **Benn & Cronin traffic indicators graced many L&Y suburban stations:** Failsworth was no exception. This example stood inside the booking hall with a Nestle's chocolate vending machine alongside. Advertisers were quick to take advantage of any space available: Edison electric light bulbs in this case. The advertisement fills a space between Up and Down timetables. Through the door way and turning right would bring the public out on to Hardman Lane; turning left along the subway brought the public to the down platform. The exceptionally neat and well-swept surroundings have been arranged for the official photographer.

Author's Collection

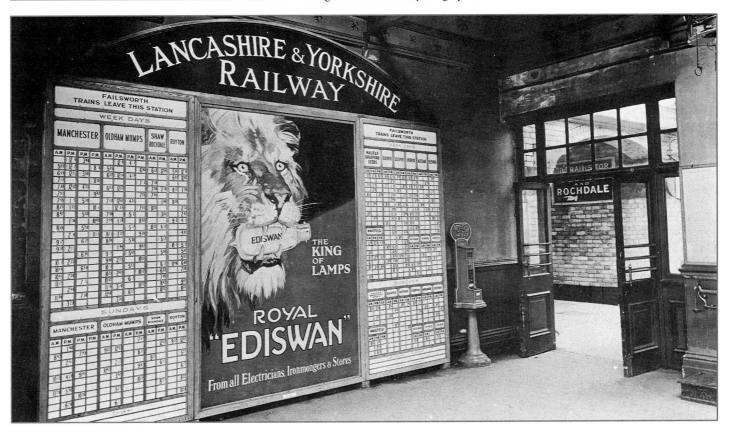

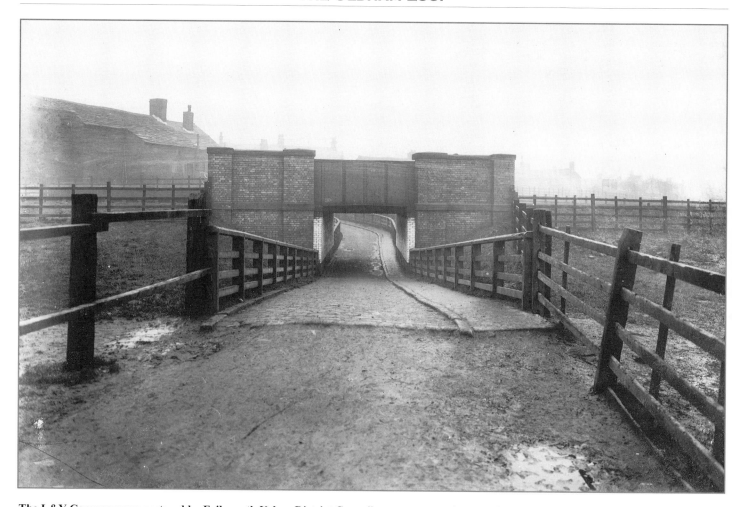

The L&Y Company was pestered by Failsworth Urban District Council to construct a subway or footbridge at Wrigley Head where a lane crossed the railway on the level. The Manchester Guardian, 14 September 1880, reported a fatal accident at the level crossing, the first on the Branch, and one involving a female fish vendor. A second accident at the crossing occurred on 30 August 1883 to two young brothers who were hit by an Up train as they returned to their home in New Moston. The L&Y eventually relented and issued a contract for the construction of a subway on 7 May 1884. The end result was photographed on 31 January1910. At this time the lane was unmade until within a short distance of the subway whereupon stone setts (lonkeys) have been used to create a metalled surface. The provision of white glazed bricks for the abutments was an extra concession to the safety of the public using an unlit right of way.

Technical Services Dept - Manchester City Council

FAILSWORTH

The Branch crossed the Rochdale Canal but once between Newton Heath and Werneth. Bridge No 20 had a skew span of 60ft and carried the railway obliquely over the canal at Wrigley Head, Failsworth. This photograph, taken in October 1995, shows the simple wrought iron girder bridge was supported on a substantial stone abutment at each end. The canal towpath is in good condition which is more than can be said for the canal whose prospect for navigation looks uncertain.

Author

Hollinwood, 25 June 1966. Although Eric Blakey's purpose was to record as many ex-L&Y details as possible at Hollinwood station, he could not resist focussing his camera at the double headed holiday special entering the station the Down line. The middle Saturday of the local Wakes fortnight provided traffic aplenty; here we see Special 1J29 hauled by pilot engine **44949** (26A Newton Heath) and sister Class 5 past the complex which constituted the electricity distribution plant owned by Ferranti Ltd. On occasions, the testing of the transformers by passing high tension electricity through them necessitated a surge of power so great that the CEGB had to be forewarned. Hollinwood station lay close to and between the two Ferranti works.
E Blakey courtesy LYRS Collection

HOLLINWOOD

Until recently Hollinwood had been a forgotten part of Oldham. Its streets, houses, shops, mills, and the urban fabric generally, all bore the dismal face of municipal neglect. It was though the local authority planners couldn't decide what to do with an area so run down as to rank as one of the twilight zones of the town. A walk along Bower Lane towards Hollinwood station from Manchester Road led the visitor to a low-headroom bridge which carried the railway up to Werneth. It was below this bridge that the narrow lane struggled to accommodate the heavy traffic which used the lane, it being a small section of the main route to Liverpool! The tallest vehicles occasionally became wedged under the low girders of the bridge despite the low-headroom warning at either end. The flagged pavements were also narrow and in wet weather were covered with a filthy slime which continuously ran down the brick abutments of the bridge, the crumbling brickwork of which, patched up in places, added to the down-at-heal character of Hollinwood.

The railway came to Hollinwood between 1875 and 1880. Its completion was regarded by residents, mill owners, and the public at large as a break-through in communications, firmly connecting the place with the outside world. In 1894 a small com-

plex railway infrastructure lay between Hudson Street to the south of the station and Drury Lane to the north of the goods station. The brick and timber passenger station had up and down platforms, its booking office entrance facing Railway Road. The latter was originally a private road running at right-angles to Bower Lane and linking it to Hudson Street. Railway Road was owned by the LYR and the LMS and up to 1948, by-laws permitted the railway companies to close the road to the public on one Sunday in the year. Once inside the brick booking hall, the intending traveller could reach the platforms by following a dingy subway from which a flight of stairs ascended to each. Both platforms extended over Bower Lane, with the signal box mounted on the up platform perched almost directly above the busy thoroughfare.

Hollinwood Goods Station lay on the eastern side of the running lines. The yard had three access points by road: Mill Lane (off Bower Lane), Clowes Street (the main access), and Drury Lane, at the northern end. The goods station handled incoming supplies of raw materials and fuel, such as cotton and coal respectively. Reference to the 1922 OS 25in plan shows that very little change had occurred since 1900, save for the laying of an array of sidings on the down side, south of the station. A contract adver-

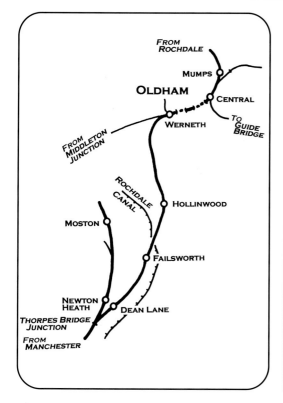

Len Higham (left) and colleague inspect a strip of garden at the Werneth end of the up platform, 24 October 1962. The low bushes were planted in tubs made by cutting old hickory shunting poles into the required lengths, splitting them, and arranging them to form a tub. The station signal box was mounted on the platform and was a late-comer to the station. Opened as LY 226 in 1913 it replaced an 1880 vintage box which had been sited on the down side, 120 yards nearer to Werneth. The 1913 box housed an L&Y 48 lever frame which controlled signalling and points, and an 8 lever ground frame at the Failsworth end of the station. The signal box was closed on 26 June 1994. ***Author's Collection***

HOLLINWOOD

tisement appeared for these on 4 July 1913. These sidings could be reached by lorries and carts from Hudson Street. Six sidings were arranged to enable road vehicles to travel alongside the rows of wagons for unloading purposes. It was a large yard with a capacity of almost 400 wagons. From the up side the short Lamont Siding received one coal wagon a week for Ferranti Ltd's boiler house.

Dominating the industrial scene was the Ferranti factory which expanded its domain with a new transformer division in 1950 by building new premises along Hollinwood Avenue. It was from this factory that large transformers were delivered by rail to customers. To witness one of these giant devices being transported by rail or road was an eye-catching experience, although the rail-borne transport was carried out at night, out of public gaze. Graham Nixon, a local resident, knew the Hollinwood area well and described their transfer by rail using special wagons: he has described the procedure as follows: *"The transformers were carried in between two longitudinal beams of the centre cradle, the ends of which were mounted on multiple-axle trolleys. These vehicles, the largest of which were rated at 135 tons had cradles which could be slewed 12 inches either side of the centre-line so as to avoid obstructions if the load was out of gauge.... such movements usually departed Hollinwood late Saturday nights or early Sunday mornings".* To effect these transfers, a seventh siding left the other six (of the 1913/4 sidings) and penetrated the eastern end of the factory.

I well remember the railway scene at Hollinwood. Shunting seemed to go on incessantly, backwards and forwards along loops 3,4 and 5 which ran behind the up platform, from the goods yard and to the shunt limit just beyond Hudson Street. The abiding images are the shabby weather-boarded station buildings, the dimly-lit signal box, the distinctive aroma emanating from the Ferranti tubing factory, and the gloomy wet decay beneath Bridge No. 26 - Bower Lane Bridge.

So drab was the station and its surroundings that an effort to brighten up the amenity was made by promoting station garden competitions. The Oldham Chronicle's "Northern Scrapbook", 8 November 1963, referred to the subject under the title *"Hollinwood Tops the Stations"*: *"From all the stations in East Lancashire, Hollinwood has won the special class award and shield in the best-kept stations competitions. In addition, a third-class award has been gained for cleanliness and tidiness in the industrial group............. The slogan, 'Hollinwood for Industry', set in clusters of white rock flowers along the platform was part of the design. Last year the station won the second award for the best-kept station garden, and the first prize for cleanliness".*

Once upon the platforms the traveller experienced some alleviation from the drabness of the area, particularly in the summer. From the streets outside, it was a different picture.

A BR Standard 4-6-0 takes one of the sidings as it crosses Bower Lane bridge, and heads for the goods yard on the northern side of the station. The road junction is that of Bower Lane and Railway Road. This is a view I recall with nostalgia; it is the corner I turned as I walked home with my parents from the Queens Cinema - one of the high spots of Hollinwood. On dark evenings the signal box was faintly lit by meagre gas lamps - someone's place of work on Saturday evenings. In 1958, a short while after Supermac had told us that we had never had it so good, Grange-over-Sands and Barrow could be reached by rail for 11/3 and 14/- (56p and 70p respectively). The train departed at 9.42 a.m. from Hollinwood. Above the BR poster, the hoarding advertises Sunblest bread - fresh to the last slice. On the Hollinwood Avenue side of the bridge a number 56 bus has turned for its return journey to Victoria Avenue/Rochdale Road terminus. Date of photograph: 2 October 1958. *Author's Collection*

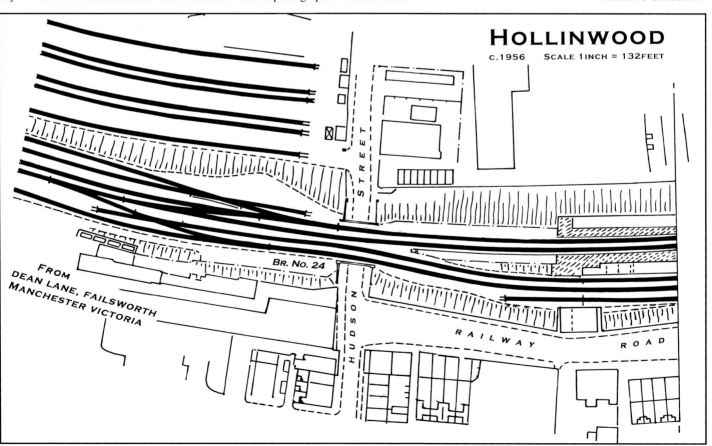

Vaguely remembered and now sorely missed - the station frontage on Railway Road. The soot-laden atmosphere has discoloured the yellow brickwork and blackened the stone dressings, but the overall solid, lightly decorated building proudly stands with its attractive awning over the half-open door way. Bargain travel enticed the public to catch the 10.39am train to Southport on the 26 June, while a no-nonsense BR(LMR) sign prohibits parking in the loading area. In 1966 there were fewer privately-owned cars to congest Railway Road, and many more parcels passing through the station door way. Photographed by *Eric Blakey* on 25 June 1966.

(Right) Well lit by the photographer's flash unit, the station subway surrenders its most intimate details. Starting at roof level are the ornate cast iron beams which took the weight of overhead trains, while further beams can be seen nearer the front entrance bearing the weight of the sidings. A modicum of daylight managed to penetrate the glass panelling laid between the tracks but the illumination was poor. The glazed white brickwork was an attempt to lighten the subway but the walls are stained and filthy after years of neglect. A notice attached to the wall reads **Trains for Oldham and Rochdale**, the indication being that the subway steps to the down platform are behind the camera. The entrance to steps leading to the up platform is on the left-hand side. The paved floor is wet, a wetness carried in by the feet of the public from the rain-soaked streets. Date of photograph: 8 October 1958. ***Author's Collection***

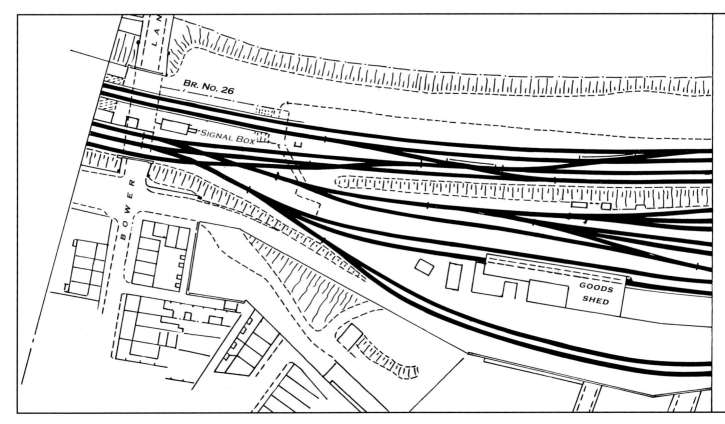

Railway Road/Bower Lane junction on 25 June 1966. By this date transport officials had erected an extra road sign depicting an arrow pointing to the old warning sign tucked away in the shadow of the bridge. The frequent number of collisions with the bridge had necessitated this eye-catching notice. Above the sloping bank, on the over the sidings, stands the Up platform, a weather board edifice fringed with a slotted valance and surmounted by a glazed roof. Electrification was the new mode of travel between Manchester and London in the 1960s - the poster announces that rail travel between the cities could be achieved in 2 hours 35 minutes. This schedule would have been remarkable in the swinging sixties, and so was High Speed Gas (natural gas), the heat that obeys you. *Eric Blakey LYRS Collection*

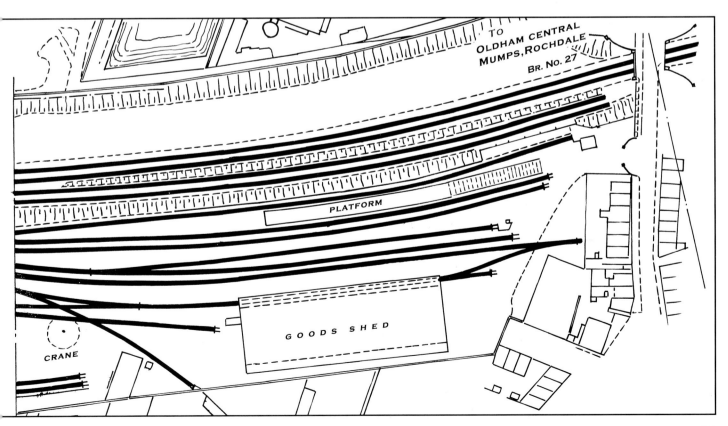

This **October 1958** view of the Manchester end of the station shows the subway roof skylights and the heavy timber longitudinal beams which bore the weight of the rails in the absence of sleepers. The Up platform stretched towards Failsworth and was bordered by a timber fence, an essential requirement where running lines and sidings lay behind the platform. Rising out of the cess at intervals, alongside the platform wall, were short wooden posts. These carried signal wires on pulleys from signal box to semaphore signals. The drab platform scene shown in this view can be compared with the horticultural enterprise of 1964. The industrial skyline was dominated by the roof line of the old Ferranti factory.   *Author's Collection*

(Right-centre) The only brick building at the station stood on the Up platform close to the signal box. It was a square L&Y vintage building forming the lamp room in which the porter or lamp man filled a variety of paraffin-burning lamps with the vital liquid. The oil was inflammable; a careless spark would have been enough to ignite the smallest of spillage. Hence the reason for the lamp room occupying an isolated site, well away from the timber buildings. Despite this safety provision, the platform at this point was surfaced with timber and supported on timber baulks. The lamp room stood above Bower Lane; the metal parapet is just visible through the gaps in the fence. When photographed on 25 June 1966 the structure had assumed a distinctive lean.
Eric Blakey; LYRS Collection

HOLLINWOOD

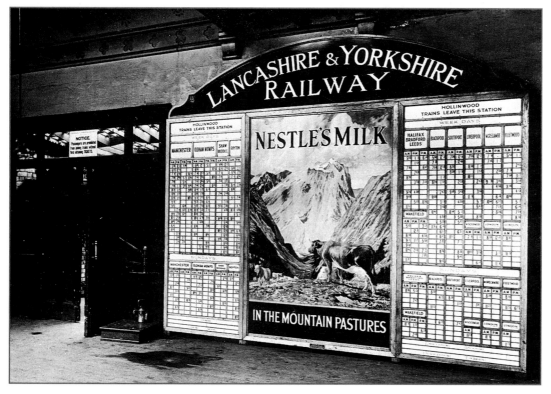

At the rear of the booking hall to the right of the subway entrance stands a Benn & Cronin indicator. This photograph was taken with only the daylight through the roof to provide a clear view. The dimness below the roof and the darkness of the nooks and crannies reveal that the interior was starved of light. Over the subway doors a notice warns that Passengers are prohibited from joining trains without first obtaining tickets. Behind the open door is an unidentified machine on whose base stands a paraffin lamp. Examples listed on the indicator show that it was possible to reach a variety of destinations even though this might involve changing trains at Victoria. Blackpool, Morecambe, Liverpool, Wakefield, and London are included, to name but a few.
Author's Collection

Hollinwood station on 30 August 1964. Len Higham, who was the Station Master at the time, had much to be proud of in the efforts administered in creating a picturesque station by means of well-tended garden plots. The plots were arranged on both platforms using stone chippings and rockery. This view was taken towards Werneth with the inescapable backcloth of spinning mills, their chimneys, and the roof tops of terraced houses and other buildings.   *Len Higham*

(Right-centre) Hollinwood was undoubtedly the centre-piece of the Branch and possessed many features of interest. This view shows the narrow-width Bower Lane passing under a low headroom bridge (No.26) which has a limited height of 13ft 3ins. A small notice attached to the parapet read **Double Deck Buses Must Not Pass Under This Bridge**, a warning issued by the Manchester Corporation Transport Department. Bower Lane constituted the eastern section of the B6393, Hollinwood Avenue, linking with the arterial A62 road between Manchester and Oldham. A small portion of the timber Down platform building of the station can be seen to the right of the bridge, and an even smaller portion of Hollinwood signal box. On a wet 2 October 1958 the British Railways poster advertises that the Blackpool Illuminations could be reached from Hollinwood station at 7 shillings (35p) return.
Authors collection

Many drivers of high vehicles were caught out by the low headroom. Having missed or ignored the signs, drivers found their vehicles trapped under the girders following a disturbing crunch of metal, with the only means of escape by letting down the tyres! Bridge 26 had a span of 32ft 6ins, was low in height as well as long in coverage of Bower Lane. This view shows the wrought iron girders beneath the main running lines and the equally low girders of the sidings beyond. Work was carried out in 1895 to give the bridge greater strength. A solitary electric street lamp provided a mean glimmer of light in an otherwise wet, grimy, and thoroughly unpleasant stretch of Bower Lane. The turning to the left is Mill Street, one of the three entrances to Hollinwood Goods Yard.   Date of photograph: 2 October 1958.
Author's Collection

Views of Hollinwood Goods Yard and associated buildings are uncommon. We are treated here to a rare picture of the sidings behind the station building, lamp room, and signal box. Readers with exceptionally good eyesight, or with the aid of a glass, will be able to discern the tender of an Ivatt 2-6-0 shunting in the yard. A siding signal arm is raised and the points set for the shunt to reverse, cross one siding, and take the middle road towards Hudson Street bridge. The sidings were laid at a lower level than the main running lines and can be seen rising up alongside the yard to meet the latter. In the far distance, at the top end of the yard, stood the three-storey, twin-gabled brick warehouse, built by Messrs E Taylor (contractor) for £24,395 in 1884.

Author's Collection

HOLLINWOOD

On 30 April 1955 Stanier 2-6-4T 42569 brings the 14.36 Victoria to Oldham stopping train round the steeply-graded portion of the Branch, between the 5¾ and 6 mile posts, at Block Lane, Chadderton. By the time the train reaches Werneth station, it will have gained a vertical height of 267 feet over a distance of 6¼ miles. The view to the west from the railway at this location provides an urban panorama, taking in Chadderton, Royton, and the lower flanks of Oldham west, relieved by Tandle Hill - a rounded eminence rising to over 600 feet above sea level. Nearer to hand, two of Chadderton's many cotton mills press up to the railway, the Mona and Ramsey mills were built in 1902.

Graham Whitehead

Featherstall Road South (Bridge No. 10) 28 May 1968. Platt's main office lay on the south side of the railway and dominated this view taken from outside the entrance to the mineral yard. The brick parapet marks the position of Platt's private sidings; the wrought iron parapet spanned the main lines. At some time both parapets have been heightened by a length of timber boarding, a feature repeated on the station side. One photograph shows stop signals affixed to the parapet; with the closure of the Werneth Incline, these signals became redundant and were removed on 10 May 1964. ***BR (LMR)***

THE IMPACT OF PLATT BROTHERS LTD; OLDHAM

The district of Greenacres lies to the east of Mumps. In the 1830s it was described by R H Eastham (Platt's Textile Machinery Makers, 1994) as *"a locality which was becoming widely industrialised"* the green acres from which the district drew its name then still largely untouched. From the confined premises at Ferney Bank, the firm found that a cotton mill in the area sufficed in its early bid for expansion. Thereafter it quickly established itself as a major textile machine manufactory, trading under the name of Hibbert, Platt & Sons. With the addition of new buildings the enterprise formed a hive of industry on the eastern outskirts of the town. One of Henry Platt's sons, John, had been a keen promoter of railways in Oldham, being sometime both a director of the LNWR and chairman of the OAGB. It is not surprising that the Company's works at Greenacres and at Werneth took advantage of the new mode of transport.

Hartford Sidings (also known as Lower Moor Sidings) were laid by the LYR on the up side of the Oldham to Rochdale line, probably opening on the same day as the opening of the line - on 3 November 1863. Certainly, by October 1871 a contract or a warehouse appeared in the Manchester Guardian. According to Company Minutes there were problems with the building of this

warehouse, the contractor, Messrs Wade, appeared to be "proceeding slowly" in October 1872, following an unexplained standstill. The completed yard could accommodate up to 226 wagons; the LYR found it necessary to open Hartford Siding signal box at the junction of the sidings and the main line in 1901. A large brick warehouse was constructed by C Brierley after securing the contract for the work on 13 May 1884.

As early as March 1865 Platt Bros. & Co. obtained a siding agreement with the LYR. This entailed one siding which left Hartford Sidings to cross Derker Street in order to enter the Works. A 25in OS plan of 1932 shows that the "goods and mineral station" which designated Hartford Sidings, was so arranged that each pair of sidings were separated by a cartway to allow horse-drawn carts and motor lurries to be loaded directly from the lines of wagons. The same plan shows that once across Derker Street the private line spread through Platt's yards with branches into various workshops. The private line continued across Bower Street and into another Works' building.

The concern also occupied an extensive area of land at Werneth where the Company opened its Hartford New Works in 1844, two years after the branch line from Middleton Junction

Featherstall Road South linked Werneth with Royton. The rise in the road near Platt's office block (the building with clock tower) was formed to provide headroom for the railway: the wrought iron parapet, the arched opening to the footbridge, and the bevy of station signs mark the spot where the railway passed beneath. Far left, a gate post and curved kerb indicate the entrance to Werneth Mineral Yard. A "C" registered car approaches the photographer whilst an Oldham Corporation bus heads towards Werneth Fire Station. Date of photograph: 28 May 1968. ***BR(LMR)***

was opened. Agreement with the Manchester & Leeds Railway for a siding was obtained as early as 1839, well in advance of the completion of the Oldham Branch. Platt's sidings were located on the down side of the Oldham Branch a short distance from Werneth station. According to Eastham, *".... the siding at Hartford New Works was a loop line which left the main line..... at a point on the gradient which ran alongside the New Works, and rejoined at Werneth station"*.

A set of dead-end sidings was positioned on the down side adjacent to the station. The sidings butted up to the retaining wall of Featherstall Road South and were for the exclusive use of Platt Bros. South of the junction of the Oldham Branch and the Hollinwood line was an unusual zig-zag arrangement situated on the down side. This permitted goods trains to leave the down line and by a series of movements, enter the Work's yard at Hartford Forge..

Hartford Iron Works was also served by a complex layout of sidings which crossed Arkwright Street several times in order to reach the inner portions of the Works. Superimposed on this layout the Company laid out a narrow gauge system in 1887 upon which a number of 0-4-0 tank engines worked industriously

shunting wagons of coal, coke, pig iron, and timber around the Works. Finished products emerged from the workshops in privately owned wagons back to the main siding which lay close to the steeply-graded (1 in 27) approach to Werneth station. R H Eastham knew the arrangements well and wrote that *"The sets of private railway sidings installed at the Platt Bros. & Co.'s two works were, by far, the most extensive in Oldham, that at Werneth being virtually a miniature railway in itself"*.

As early as 1868 the firm assumed the mantle of a limited liability company. Gradually the head-quarters were transferred to Werneth and the name "New Works" was dropped so that the name was abbreviated to Hartford Works. The old works at Greenacres was re-named East Works. Hartford Sidings were closed on 2 November 1970. Passengers leaving Mumps and Werneth stations for Hollinwood and Manchester pass through the vestiges of Platt's Werneth empire, now mostly ruins of the former industrial complex. Notwithstanding the unpleasant squealing of the flanges of the Class 142 Pacer units as the train negotiates the tight curve, there is a fine view on the left of an imposing building which declares to the world "Hartford Iron Works".

An excellent view from the Up platform at Werneth station in May 1964. The junction was at the meeting of the Hollinwood Branch and the Werneth Incline route from Middleton Junction. The former was at a higher level and swung across to join the steeply-graded (1 in 27) incline. So steep was the gradient that special precautions were in place affecting goods trains. A notice board near the stone pier exhorts drivers to *Stop and pin down brakes.* Werneth had its complement of bridges. The oldest was the 25ft span (right) which accommodated two of Platt Bros. sidings. Cast iron beams forming the bridge display their origin by the embossed words R Ormerod & Son, Manchester 1842. Platt Bros. maintained this section of bridge. The 49ft span to the left carried Featherstall Road South - one of Oldham's principal highways. Extending towards Werneth station was the wrought iron lattice footbridge (No.11) which linked the public road with the station footbridge (No.12), whose dark underside appears at the top of the photograph.

T A Fletcher

OLDHAM WERNETH

A quiet moment at Werneth recorded on 20 November 1956. Two railway employees stand on the dirt path which past between the complex of point-rodding and signal wires, and the signal box garden. Bridge 12 stands as built by the L&Y: the Company never numbered its bridges so that the number plate affixed to the pier is an LMS provision. The overline footbridge had a span of 31ft and was made up of wrought iron girders, lattice work, and floorplates. It was strengthened in 1879. A ground disc signal standing alongside the down line points controlled setting-back movements over the cross-over to the up line.

BR (LMR)

The western approach to the station could be observed by poking the head through the window of a train coming off the Hollinwood Branch. The date is 12 April 1957 when much of the infrastructure was still in place. Several features deserve our attention, not least Werneth Station signal box. This was opened between 1931 and 1933, and located on the Up side at a point 25 yards west of an earlier L&Y box (LY 225) of 1900 vintage. The replacement box was of LMS design and in 1966 housed 28 levers (24w 4s) and worked from 5 a.m. to 11.25 p.m., Monday to Saturday. It was closed on 21 May 1967. Werneth station goods shed, partly hidden by smoke in this view, appears on the right, very much out of use and bereft of the tracks which served it. A small rectangular sign just above ground level marks a boundary between OLDHAM DISTRICT and MANCHESTER DISTRICT. Ahead of the locomotive we have a good view through the station to Werneth Tunnel.   *H C Casserley*

OLDHAM WERNETH

(Right-centre) The first station to serve Oldham was opened for passengers by the Manchester & Leeds Railway on 31 March 1842. During the previous month the Manchester Guardian (26 February) reported that *The building of the station at Oldham has been let to Messrs Pearson & Smith and is proceeding with much spirit.* Fast work indeed. The appellation Werneth was adopted when Oldham Mumps station opened in 1849. This view shows the original M&L station building which spanned the line and later to become Bridge 13. It was supported in the centre by four cast iron columns with jack arches forming the underside. The front of the station faced a setted approach road leading off Railway Road, a prosaic building with little architectural merit. The platforms were originally covered by a train shed roof, but this photograph shows the final result of the L&Y's spate of station rebuilding between 1880 and 1895. Rebuilding was piecemeal; new waiting rooms, for example, were added to the up side in 1882. Careful study of the wall facing the camera reveals the outline of the overall roof and a sealed window. The remaining windows, at different levels, appear to have been added after the removal of the roof. Glazed platform canopies are supported on thick timber baulks resting on cast iron columns which exhibit a flourish of ornamentation. Beyond the station lay Werneth Tunnel, 471 yards long.   *Jim Cocker*

Werneth station viewed beneath the overhead station building and looking towards the Up platform. This is a rare sunny picture taken in 1964: most views show the station and its environs during dull weather which added to the dismal character of the location. At the far end of the Up platform are the waiting rooms, staff quarters and offices. A number of people gathers outside these rooms, perhaps awaiting a train. The footbridge doubled as a signal bridge: in 1964 only the left-hand signal was in use for traffic following the Hollinwood Branch. The former route to Middleton Junction is out of use and has been fenced off. A Werneth feline wanders towards the platform edge, and peace reigns at the station.   *Oldham Evening Chronicle*

The clock in Platt's office tower gives the time as 12.32pm. The photographer has moved to the Down platform to capture this scene looking west towards the junction. The difference in the 1 in 27 and 1 in 44 gradients of both routes as they leave the station is clearly seen. Although barely visible after years of soot deposits, two notices attached to the road bridge parapet warn drivers of goods trains to pin down brakes before descending the inclines. Equivalent signs were later placed at track level. The 'bobby' has just departed his box and is walking along the path towards the station, swinging a water can. Lack of space forced the S&T to erect the Up stop signals on the bridge - both are track-circuited, meaning that they are exempt from Rule 55. At the end of the Up platform is a Hawkes-eye station sign, named after the designer G C Hawkes who introduced the sign for the LMS

in 1934. This scene belongs to an age of grime and unabashed neglect on British railways; an age of Rock n' Roll, Bill Haley and the Comets, 'Teddy' boys, and a world caught up in the Suez Crisis.   ***BR (LMR)***

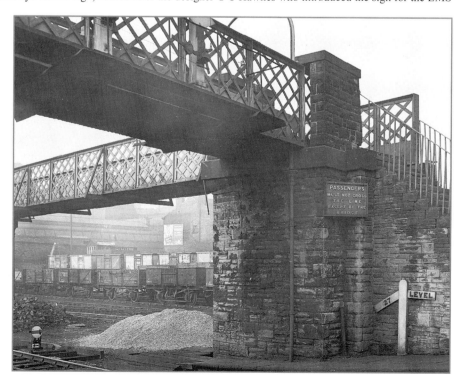

(Right-lower) A close-up of Bridge 12 from the station showing the series of steps leading to the Down platform. Bridge 11 constituted the lattice footbridge which gave passengers direct access to the station from Featherstall Road South. There were three spans separated by cast iron columns between the road entrance and the stone pier: these measured 62ft 6ins, 72ft 6ins, and 61ft. Platt's siding is well-stocked with coal wagons - a mixture of older plank wagons and 1950s steel 16 ton version. Against the retaining wall stands a coal merchant's cabin, occupied at this time by J E Southern & Co. Ltd. Of interest is the well-known gradient post which signified the level stretch through the station, and the 1 in 27 fall towards Middleton Junction. Perched diagonally on the bridge pier is a wooden L&Y station sign depicting a familiar prohibition. Today, such signs fetch a considerable sum of money at auctions. The end wall of a nearby building informs the world of Scott's Porridge oats, and that You can't beat Woodbine cigarettes for flavour and satisfaction.   ***BR(LMR)***

AN INDUSTRIAL TRIO

Platt Bros.' extensive sidings at both their works necessitated the use of a fleet of locomotives for internal shunting. The earliest of these were built by the Dukinfield firm of Daniel Adamson & Co., but information about them is sketchy and often conflicting. Most, if not all, were 0-4-0 side tanks with steeply inclined outside cylinders (12ins by 14 ins) and 3ft 10ins wheels. Several were sold to the government during the Great War. Later locomotives were all 0-4-0 saddle tanks, all of them new to Platt's. Two are illustrated here. The *upper (left)* photograph shows *Werneth* standing on its home ground at the new works. *Werneth* was manufactured by Hawthorn Leslie in 1923, and was scrapped in 1958. The other saddle tank *(above-right)* is *Coldhurst* at the East Works, another Hawthorn Leslie dating back to 1899. It was scrapped in 1953. The photograph to the *left* shows *Oldham*, one of the original Adamson locos, probably at the Werneth Works. Upper photographs by the late *C A Appleton*. I am grateful to *Jim Peden* for the above details and for permission to reproduce the photographs.

OLDHAM WERNETH
TRACK LAYOUT C.1956

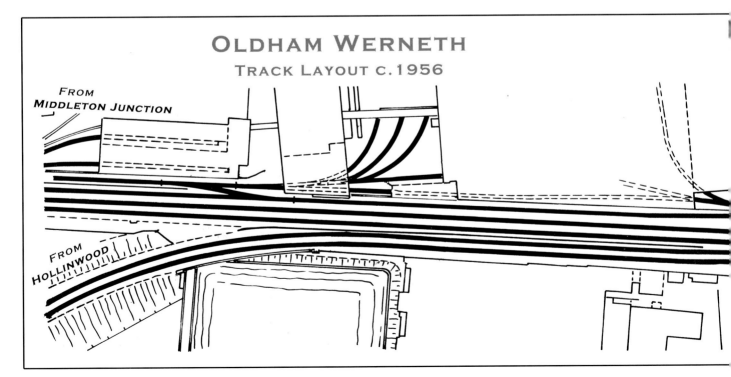

FROM
MIDDLETON JUNCTION

FROM
HOLLINWOOD

Eric Bentley stood at the western end of the Up platform at Werneth to capture this moment on film. A double-headed train surmounts the 1 in 44 gradient at the head of the Hollinwood Branch, at 10.45am on 17 June 1967. Black Fives' **44679** (8F Springs Branch) and **44905** (10A Carnforth) are in charge of the 1L10 holiday special, Failsworth to Blackpool North. The train had departed at 10.40 from Failsworth. The foot of Werneth signal box is strewn with scrap materials under BR's unofficial dump-it-anywhere scheme. Undeterred, the bold 20 sign indicates to drivers about to descend the incline that a maximum speed of 20 m.p.h. is in force. While this railway action is taking place, an Oldham Corporation bus (remember the maroon and cream livery?) heads for Oldham Road along Featherstall Road South.

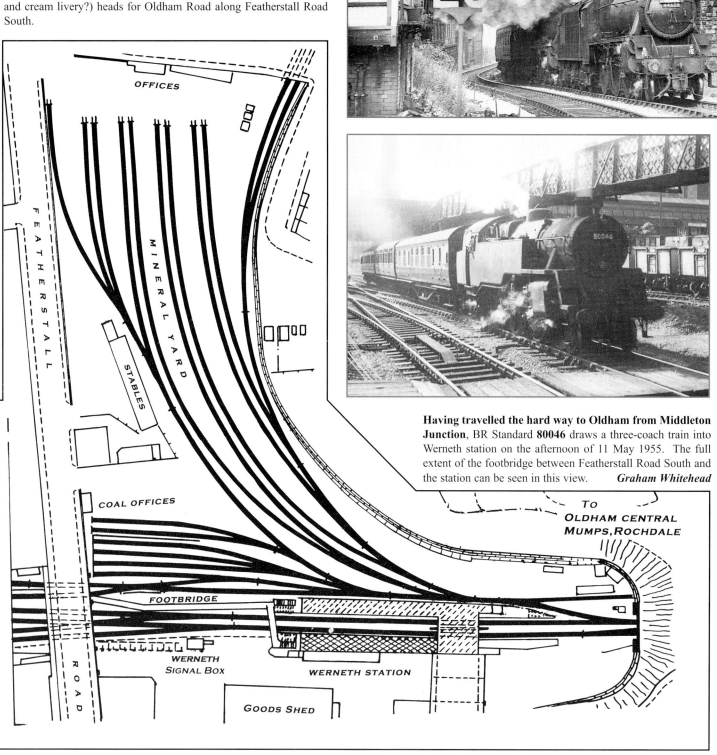

Having travelled the hard way to Oldham from Middleton Junction, BR Standard **80046** draws a three-coach train into Werneth station on the afternoon of 11 May 1955. The full extent of the footbridge between Featherstall Road South and the station can be seen in this view. *Graham Whitehead*

A grimy Stanier tank engine takes a sunlit road through Werneth station. Despite someone's attempt to clean the bunker it is difficult to be sure that the correct number is **42643**. The position of the stop signal to the right of the line to which it applies is for improved sighting purposes. Central Tunnel can be discerned beyond the far end of Werneth Tunnel. *Graham Whitehead*

OLDHAM
WERNETH

(Right-centre) **A view of the booking hall interior**, this time facing a set of stairs leading down to the Royton and Rochdale platform. Apart from the Swan Vestas advertisement there is little else to lend a modicum of brightness to the place. Such an ambience was probably acceptable in the L&Y period, greeting many thousands of passengers who passed through the station. In June 1966, when this photograph was taken, the booking hall had long passed its best.
Eric Blakey; LYRS Collection

In L&Y days the spartan interior of the station booking hall possessed a Benn & Cronin indicator. Like the example at Hollinwood, Werneth's version had a centre panel reserved for advertising, on this occasion, a bovine commodity. Observe the meagre ceiling decoration, the heavy timber beams supporting the roof, the large window, and the tongue-and-groove floor. A notice fastened to the wall had much to say under the title Lancashire & Yorkshire Railway. How many Oldhamers bothered to stand, read, and absorb the Business Line's message to passengers? The backless seat was the only concession to public comfort in an otherwise drab and cheerless room. *Author's Collection*

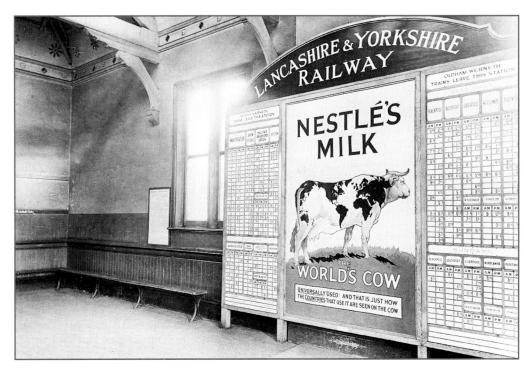

Stanier 8F 48773 (9K Bolton shed) eases a lengthy coke train through the station and on to the 1 in 44 falling gradient at the head of the Hollinwood Branch. The photograph is undated but two obvious features of change place the date sometime after 1964. One major change is at the southern end of the platforms where the junction has been removed (14 June 1964) to form a plain line leading directly to the Branch. The other obvious change is to the station footbridge: the original lattice structure was replaced with a steel box type in 1957. *Jim Cocker*

An unidentified Stanier 8F trundles through the station, tender first, with a train of mineral empties. By the mid-1960s general dilapidation had set in: the end wall of the Up side station building exhibits not only an irregular profile but also a surface of uneven brickwork with gaps to boot. With consummate optimism Nature has re-asserted herself with the growth of vegetation in the area abandoned by man. Grass and bushes have sprung up amongst the debris of bricks, concrete slabs, pieces of timber, and lengths of metal piping, etc. The reconstructed footbridge exemplifies the only promising feature in the derelict scene. *Jim Cocker*

The photographer was in time to capture what was left at Werneth on one of his photographic excursions in June 1966. His picture shows a clear view of the ground frame cabin and the small wooden coal stage behind. In L&Y days it was customary for goods trains on the Down line to enter the tunnel in order to clear the points before setting back into the coal yard on the Down side. A driver listened for the sound of a gong mounted inside the tunnel which signalled that his train could set back. The gong signal and the setting of points were operated from the ground frame. This was rendered out of action on 21 May 1967 when all connections worked by it were secured in the normal position, pending removal. Hitherto it had accommodated ten levers (7w 3s), with electric release by Werneth Station box. The high retaining wall on the left curved back and continued some distance alongside the coal yard. Without this wall the open ground, streets, and buildings would have suffered from subsidence.

Eric Blakey LYRS Collection

Stanier tank 42568 emerges from Werneth Tunnel on the up line, next stop Werneth. The train is the 7.09 p.m. stopping train bound for Manchester, photographed on 27 May 1958. Water column 226 partially hides Werneth Ground Frame, housed in a miniature cabin on a piece of land outside the tunnel. Werneth station's Down starter is off for a train routed by either the Hollinwood Branch or from Middleton Junction. This signal was track-circuited meaning that the disposition of the signal arm was electrically repeated in the signal box; this is indicated by the diamond-shaped plate attached to the signal post. Heavy stone retaining walls extended on both sides of the tunnel portal, a feature of the work carried out when the Mumps Extension line was constructed between 1845-7.

Author's Collection

On 4 August 1968, 1L50, the RCTS "Farewell to Steam" rail tour, began at London Euston bound for Manchester Victoria via Rugby. Places visited in the North West included Stockport, Oldham, Rochdale, Bury, Bolton, Blackburn, and the outskirts of Liverpool, before returning to Manchester Victoria and thence to London Euston. The special was caught on camera between Werneth and Central tunnels, Oldham, with Stanier 8F **48476** piloting BR Standard **73069**, both climbing the 1 in 80 gradient towards Mumps station. The leading engine is just about to run over catch points before plunging into Central Tunnel. *Paul Jordan, courtesy of Bernard Crick*

Smoke and steam drift out of the confines of the 449 yards long Central Tunnel - a rare view of the eastern portal. Werneth has been left behind and we approach Oldham's central area. Far left is the Up platform of Central station which extended further west than the down platform from which the photograph has been taken. The stop signal is backed by a white sighting board to make its disposition (on or off) clearer to engine crew, while splitting distants lie beneath, one of which is attached to a right-hand bracket and applying to the Up line to Middleton Junction. Lying in the 6 foot are Hallade pegs (concrete blocks) which were designed for checking the alignment of track work. Overlooking the cutting is an assemblage of industrial premises: above right is the half-demolished Welllington Mill which succumbed to the town by-pass in 1968, while above the tunnel stands Motor Bodies (Oldham) Ltd. *Graham Whitehead*

The western end of Oldham Central 12 April 1957. A fully-functioning amenity when this photograph was taken, it provides us with a picture of what the station looked like during a lull in the traffic. The ridge and furrow glazed canopies have been cut back on both sides, the one over the Down platform more than the other. Tell-tale signs of cleaner brickwork appear over the arched windows, where there has been protection from the soot-laden atmosphere. On the Down side an inclined footpath follows the line of the retaining wall, its lower end leading pedestrians on to the platform. The imposing building with a hipped roof is the booking and parcels office, which has a frontage at the corner of Clegg Street and Wellington Street. Interchange between platforms could be made by a footbridge alongside Clegg Street; this can be seen in front of the arched bridge (No.18) carrying Clegg Street proper.

H C Casserley

(Left) From Clegg Street bridge, Eric Blakey photographed Central on 25 June 1966, four weeks and five days after the station had closed. The high vantage point gives a fine study of the ridge and furrow roof style of the platform canopy. Even from this angle it is possible to see the clean brickwork which had been protected by the canopy before its removal. The uncovered stretch of the Down platform already has a carpet of vegetation spilling down from the cutting and taking root in and around a former station garden.

LYRS Collection

By moving several yards nearer the platform canopy - opposite (upper) - the photographer has treated us to an even clearer view of the L&Y cast iron-work, characterised in this instance by ever decreasing circles pattern. We can also see in more detail the alterations made to Clegg Street bridge. LMS Bridge Records indicate that the 38ft span arched bridge was widened on each side with the use of wrought iron girders to accommodate footpaths on either side of the street. The eastern girder was replaced in steel in 1942 and encased in concrete. A new brick parapet was constructed on the western side. Beyond the bridge is it possible to see Rhodes Bank footbridge, Waterloo Sidings signal box, and the tail end of a passenger train entering Clegg Street station. As already mentioned in a previous caption, the Up platform extended further west than the down. This photograph shows the opposite to hold, in effect the station having overlapping platforms. Date of photograph: 1958.   *G H Platt*

Central station booking and parcels office on 25 June 1966, several weeks after closure (closed, 18 April 1966). The building was still intact, although looking somewhat forlorn - a discarded amenity on the edge of the town centre. The view is towards the south east with the tall side archway facing on to Clegg Street. A small portion of the renewed brick parapet of Bridge 18 nudges on to the photograph, extreme left. The gate at the far end of the porch marks the position of the inclined passage which leads to the Down platform. Unpretentious in character, the building actually stood in a recess of Wellington Street where parking was available and the loading/unloading of railway vehicles could be undertaken. A notice by the side of the main door warns the public to BEWARE OF PICKPOCKETS.
Eric Blakey LYRS

Central station booking office interior in L&Y days. The focus of interest is the Benn & Cronin indicator which was more than adequate for informing the public the times of trains. Standing on the wooden floor near the window is a notice board, in front of which lies a wicker basket tied with string, with label attached. Joseph Bridge, the Passenger Agent, had his own office, a door mat obliging visitors to wipe their feet before entering the inner sanctum. One of the ticket-issuing windows has a message dangling from a pin - perhaps an L&Y version of 'position closed'. On the wall between the two ticket windows a notice board presents the L&Y's rules and regulations - something to read while waiting for the train. ***Author's Collection***

OLDHAM CENTRAL

Light and dark on a sunlit day in 1955. This view of an unidentified "Crab" heading for Central Tunnel was taken in the shadow of Clegg Street bridge form the Down platform. This side of the station is deserted, a reflection of the many quiet moments between trains out of the peak hours. ***Graham Whitehead***

Stanier 'Black Five' 45420 (9D Buxton shed) opens her safety valve whilst passing the site of Central station to pick up an evening parcel train from Oldham Parcel Concentration Depot. This particular loco was manufactured by W G Armstrong Whitworth & Co. Ltd., one of 227 Black Fives built by the company and delivered between August 1936 and December 1937. **45420** was built to Lot 131, Works No.1475, in October 1937. It had not long to steam up for it was withdrawn in June 1968; the photograph was taken on 20 June! As already mentioned, the station was closed to the public on 18 April 1966 - two years on, the building has been obliterated from the scene. ***Peter Hutchinson***

Oldham Central on a sunny day in April 1957. Fairburn class 4MT No **42289** pulls out of the station with a Victoria to Rochdale train, next stop Mumps. The photograph was taken by Jim Davenport from the Up platform of Clegg Street station, and taking centre stage is the upper floor (street level) of Central's booking office and the neighbouring Railway and Central Hotel. By 1957 the S&T Department had installed colour light signals with 3-way stencil type route indicators at Clegg Street, although semaphore signalling still held its own. One unusual feature is marked by the signal post (No. 22) without an arm, standing at the end of the Down platform. A reference to this is made in the 1947 Section C notices in which an description of the signal is given: Commencing at 8.30am Friday, June 20, a temporary outer home signal fixed at the end of Oldham (Cen) Station Down platform will be brought into use, and will remain in use until 8.30am on Monday, June 30. During the Wakes holidays, Mumps No. 1 box had control over this signal, its purpose being to shorten the section between Werneth box and Mumps No. 1 to effect speedier despatch of trains between Werneth and Mumps stations. The last reference to this procedure was made in 1963.   *Jim Davenport, courtesy B K B Green*

The close proximity of Clegg Street (left) and Central (right) stations is illustrated quite graphically in this view west from the Up platform of the former station. For an independent company as small as the OA&GB, it's facilities at each end of the line were modestly impressive. The other company of the partnership in it's early days however, the LNW&R, was not averse to a little one-upmanship in the timetabling of passenger trains. Whereas the fifty-odd or so daily MS&L trains were allowed two minutes journey time for the half mile between Clegg Street and Glodwick Road, the forty-plus of the L&NWR could do it on just one!   *G H Platt*

Stanier 2-6-2T 40081 leaves Clegg Street with the 14.02 service to Ashton (Oldham Road), 11 May 1955. The photograph has been taken overlooking the southern end of the station from the higher level section of Clegg Street goods station. Beyond is Sheepwashers Tunnel (in reality a covered way) over which five sidings extended towards Central Tunnel. Forming the background is the LNWR goods warehouse, unmistakable for its four enclosed hoists and distinctive curvature. In 1955 the building still served a purpose - today, it languishes pending a decision about its future. The area once occupied by the station, goods yard and tunnel, was eventually to become the Alexandra Retail Park with but a few vestiges of its railway past extant. *Graham Whitehead*

CLEGG STREET

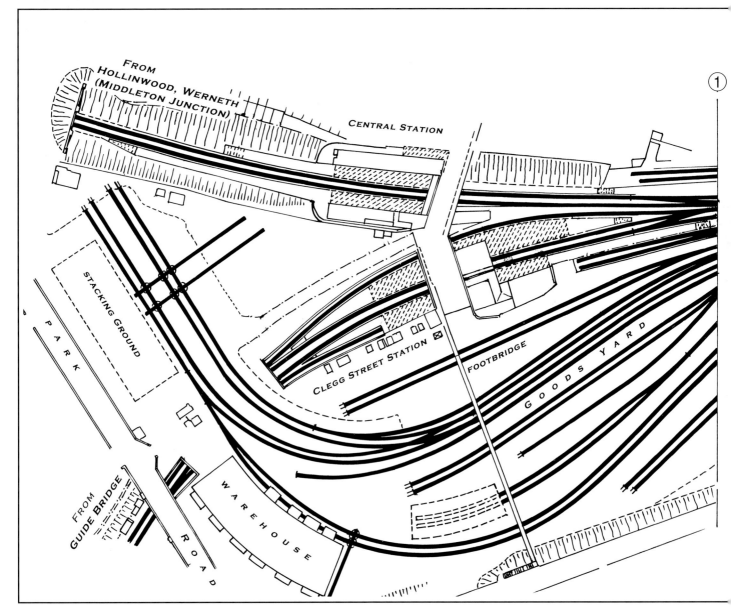

In June 1953, Jim Davenport stood on the Down platform at Clegg Street and photographed this burst of activity. 'Black Five' **45401** assists a Stanier Class 5 2-6-0 on a relief service from Llandudno, reporting number W631. The station was dominated by the church-like building which straddled the railway at the eastern end of Clegg Street. In Coronation year the fabric of the place looked reasonably cared for, with few superficial signs of deterioration, mainly broken windows. Over to the right we have a view of Central Station with its alignment curving in the opposite direction towards Central Tunnel.

Jim Davenport

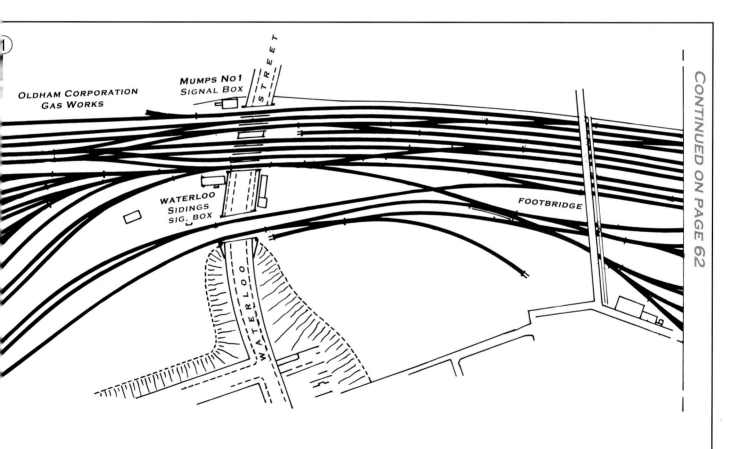

OLDHAM CORPORATION GAS WORKS

MUMPS No1 SIGNAL BOX

STREET

WATERLOO SIDINGS SIG. BOX

WATERLOO

FOOTBRIDGE

CONTINUED ON PAGE 62

OLDHAM CENTRAL · OLDHAM CLEGG STREET
TRACK LAYOUT C. 1947. 1 INCH = 132 FEET

Clegg Street station viewed from the south east. There are now signs of deterioration in the condition of the station which can be seen in this photograph taken on 12 April 1957. The station must have been a gloomy place in which to await a train at the best of times. On a wet day in December, as darkness shrouded the area in the early afternoon, it could only have been desolate and depressing. The station sign left no doubt as to where the traveller had arrived, maybe from Stockport, Guide Bridge, Ashton, and even London. The Rochdale M.P., John Bright, passed this way many times on journeys between his constituency and the House of Commons in the Metropolis. His thoughts about the station were not recorded.   *H C Casserley*

This "Running-in" nameboard, the traditional method of station identification, leaves the passenger in no doubt as to where they are. The cast-iron lettering screwed to a wooden backgound survived until the station closed in 1958.   *G H Platt*

A light fall of snow and a splash of weak sunshine combine to transform the gloom of Clegg Street into a bright and cheerful station. Nevertheless, the unglazed canopies reveal the exposed wrought iron skeleton to the sky and the wooden valance and woodwork cry out for a coat of protective paint. There would be little point in seeking shelter beneath the platform canopies during a fall of rain. Windswept and exposed, this was Clegg Street in the final years before its demise. Despite the run-down condition, the amenity continued to serve as one the town's railway passenger stations until the end. Stanier 2-6-4T **42551** furnishes the 12.42pm to Stockport, a service via Ashton which would be very welcome today. Alas, this is an unlikely possibility until total gridlock on the roads forces the issue. Pure snow lies amongst the shambles of neglect.   *Jim Davenport*

(Above) **The OA&GB provided passengers with first class facilities at its Oldham base**, but it would appear that the company's demise in 1948 signalled an end to the upkeep of Clegg Street station. This 1958 view from the east end of the station shows - to the extreme right of the picture - (Oldham) Mumps No 1 signal Box which overlooked the junction of and controlled access to and from the erstwhile L&Y and OA&GB lines. *G H Platt*

OLDHAM
CLEGG STREET

Man at work outside Clegg Street station, summer 1955. Billboards were an effective way of advertising coming events on the railways. This new one receives finals strokes to even out the wrinkles. The workman is armed with a shoulder bag in which he carries rolls of bills. A long-handled brush, and a paste bucket complted his kit.. The official uniform for the job consisted of bib-and-brace overalls, an old jacket, and customary cloth cap. The Daily Mirror's Andy Cap could have been one of is pals at the race course. August trips to Southport in 1955 cost 5/6 (27.5p) return from Mumps, Central, and Werneth. *Graham Whitehead*

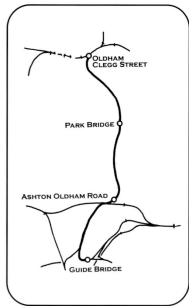

OLDHAM CLEGG STREET

Eric Blakey visited Clegg Street station on 25 June 1966 and found the premises in a very poor condition after being closed for seven years. These three views, however, show aspects of the station - those odd corners which deserve some attention. The first (**above**) looks south east towards the eastern side of the station, revealing the staircase which led from the platform to the covered footbridge and booking hall. The building to the far right constituted the parcels office, sandwiched between the two stations - a foot in both camps. We also have a rare glimpse of the inclined footbridge which linked the parcels office to station booking hall. Also in view are the goods yard lattice footbridge and a corner of Oldham P.C.D. The second photograph (**centre**) was taken from the same footbridge and looks across the station roof toward Central Gas Works. Oldham in the mid-1960s had more than its fair share of urban blight. All this was to be swept away in 1968/9 to make way for the southern by-pass. Eric Blakey took the third photograph (**right-lower**) from an elevated position above Sheepwashers 'cut-and-cover' tunnel. Points to notice include the derelict bay (bereft of track and choked with weeds), the gradual dismantling of the platforms, and the necessity for check rails along the tightly curved running lines.

We have much to be thankful for that Eric Blakey made it his mission to record as many L&Y structures as possible before they were swept away. His camera work also extended to Clegg Street goods yard which was jointly owned by the LNWR/GCR in the form of the OA&GB Junction Railway. The locally famous LNWR goods warehouse did not fail to receive his attention; here it is pictured on 25 June 1966, out of use, but still intact. The history of the building's ownership is unclear. According to a letter received by the Oldham Borough Surveyor's Office on 22 November 1875, the warehouse was designed by the MS&LR's Engineer's Office in Manchester. A set of drawings which accompanied the letter indicates that the building was originally intended to be constructed over Sheepwashers Tunnel in rectilinear form. The Oldham Chronicle, 6 May 1876, reported the stone-laying ceremony carried out by Mr Henry Morgan, the OA&GB Jct. Railway's General Manager. The memorial stone was placed under a window at the south east end; it bore the inscription: *This stone was laid by Henry Morgan Esq., Manager of the Oldham, Ashton & Guide Bridge Junction Railway, May 1st 1876.* At the conclusion of the ceremony a dinner was given at the Central Hotel, presided over by Mr Bustard, one of the contractors. The building was intended to be 253ft long by 75ft wide. It has been described as a red brick building with stone facings under a double-hipped, Queen post truss slated roof. There are four storeys from the yard level and five from the ground level on the Park Road side. The design is of the Cambrian style of architecture, unusual for its curvilinear plan shape of 330ft (five chains) radius, and including a floor space of 58,520 square yards. *LYRS Collection*

Close-up of the eastern end of the warehouse showing details of a ground floor doorway and the lower portion of the fire-escape. The latter was probably a late fixture to comply with fire regulations; the system was manufactured and erected by Messrs Joseph Hall. Two marks on, and three holes in the brickwork above the door suggest that the doorway was originally covered by an awning. The notice to the right of the loading door reads CARTERS AND OTHERS ARE WARNED NOT TO STAND UNDER THE JIGGERS - a sensible precaution when the jiggers were operating. *Eric Blakey LYRS Collection*

A section of the eastern end of the warehouse facing on to Woodstock Street. This end had a jigger, topped by an awning at roof level. The depth of the windows throughout the building decreases from ground floor to the top storey in pseudo-Georgian style. A set of internal stairs at each end enabled those inside to gain access to the different floors. At the foot of this particular photograph a single length of rail marks the position of a short siding which was connected by wagon turntables to the outer sidings. *Eric Blakey LYRS Collection*

(Left) One corner of the west-facing end of the warehouse became the study of close attention on 25 June 1966. The focus of interest were the two cast iron plates attached to the wall apprising shunters, capstan operators, and others, the regulations regarding the use of capstans. Employment of shunting horses was probable before 1900 but it is not known whether some other means, electrical or steam, was adopted in the yard at some stage. The regulations in the upper plate are there to effect safety about the yard when shunting is in progress. A further puzzle concerns the owner of the upper plate since it seems inappropriate to have L&Y regulations attached to an LNWR warehouse.

(Above) The goods warehouse seen from the western side again shows the distinctive curvature of the building, one of the features which has led to its protection as a Grade 2 listed building. Architects have studied the building closely and have described its appearance as possessing classical Georgian features such as the decreasing length of the windows with height. The concave face was symmetrically planned with four landing bays with shallow gables over, the curved angles re-inforced in blue brick. The lower corners of the building are chamfered: one of these can be seen in the photograph. The pulley at ground level was an effective method of guiding tow ropes during shunting.

(Above-centre) An example of one of the capstans in Clegg Street Goods Yard, photographed on 25 June 1966. Those readers old enough to remember the 1950s and earlier will remember that it was commonplace to see horses and drays carting all kinds of merchandise from and to goods yards. The changeover to motorised haulage required the training of drivers to handle road vehicles. An agreement between the Great Central and London & North Western Joint Committee (OA&GB Jct Railway) and the LMSR, dated 9 June 1939, granted the latter permission to use the roadways in the yard as a training ground for motor drivers. The LMSR was asked to pay £1 per year in acknowledgement, and also to pay £46 12s 0d towards the upkeep of the roadways.

The open-sided hipped-roofed tranship shed at Clegg Street Goods Yard occupied a position adjacent to the south west side of the yard footbridge, a small part of which can be seen in the left background. Despite the date (25 June 1966) the shed still houses several wagons; there is also a brake van outside the shed. This photograph gives some idea of the method of surfacing the yard - with lonkeys, or grit-stone setts - a very common method in the streets of northern towns. The chimney "disappearing" off the upper edge of the photograph belongs to Central Mill, whilst the other two eminences belong to the Star Mill on Woodstock Street.

*All: **Eric Blakey - LYRS collection***

Clegg Street Goods Yard footbridge linked Woodstock Street with Clegg Street, providing a convenient way (**top-left**) of reaching both passenger stations form the Park Road area of Oldham. Bridge No.31 (5 miles 24 chains from Stockport East Junction) was a public right of way consisting of wrought iron lattice girders supported on seven cast iron columns. It was constructed about 1875 and had a total length of 180ft. The photograph (**centre-left**) shows the arrangement of stairs which stood opposite Clegg Street station. The opposite end of the bridge terminated at a set of stone steps which led down to Woodstock Street. These steps are still there at the time of writing (December 1999). The third photograph (**above-right**) shows the top of the stairs and the first length of the bridge. The floor consisted of wrought iron buckled footplates covered with tarmacadam. Note the double cross-bracing and the ornate features on and above the columns. These were 12 inches in diameter; the height of the bridge above rail level was 15ft. *Eric Blakey LYRS Collection*

Buffer stops are not usually of great interest to photographers or to railway followers. They existed and were taken for granted as part of the scene which would always be with us. Eric Blakey left no stone unturned in his quest for a comprehensive record of railway features. These two examples were no exception; although erected to carry out the task of arresting the movement of loose wagons on the move, both have been constructed in different ways. The use of heavy timber and early bull-head rail seems common to both types. *LYRS Collection*

The ramp end of Clegg Street station formed a good vantage point to watch and photograph the passing trains to and fro between Central and Mumps stations. There seems to be plenty of activity beyond the four-coach passenger train on a Rochdale to Victoria service. BR Standard **80042** runs bunker first on the approach to Central station, past the gas works, with its third carriage level with Mumps No.1 signal box. The other box in view (far right) is Waterloo Sidings box which stood directly opposite Mumps No.1. Both were closed with the re-signalling scheme between Mumps and Werneth in 1967. *Jim Davenport*

Stanier 4MT glides down the 1 in 79 gradient on the eastern approach to Central station with a Royton to Victoria train, photographed in April 1957. Oldham is not a picturesque town; in the 1950s it was even less so. Crowding down to the northern edge of the railway was a hotchpotch of industrial premises. Central Gas Works was one of them. The Works opened in 1827 in private ownership, and by 1853 was supplying 2,170 customers. Gas manufacture ceased in 1932 but the site continued to function as offices and workshops. Close by was the Corporation refuse destructor. Those who knew speak of the sickening smell which permeated the area, emanating from the process of boiling waste into pig swill. There were other small industrial premises, cheek by jowl with each other and forming a margin of dilapidation alongside the railway. *Jim Davenport*

Standing on one of the steel girders forming Waterloo Street bridge, the photographer caught this venerable oldie engaged in a spot of shunting. Ex-L&Y Aspinall 0-6-0 52248 shunts empty stock along the up line out of Mumps station. Again, the date is unknown, but probably in the late 1950s. The locomotive was withdrawn in March 1962. Spanning the railway in the middle distance is Rhodes Bank footbridge, which is today the only surviving relic of L&Y origin.

Jim Davenport

An unidentified BR Standard 2-6-4T takes all the strain as she pilots 'Black 5' **45495** on a returning Wakes relief just outside Central station. No date is known but the assumption is that this is a June day in the late 1950s. Of interest is the two-aspect colour light signal and route indicator which applied to passenger loop line traffic through Clegg Street station. The colour lights showed caution and stop (top - yellow: bottom - red) and were deeply hooded. It is thought that this was a war-time measure aiding black out conditions. If correct, this gives some idea of how long colour lights have been installed in Oldham. The three-way route indicator acted like a destination roller used on buses. Routes indicated were, G = goods line; M = main line to Glodwick Road station; X = over crossing to LMS, that is, to Mumps station.

Stanier 2-6-4T 42551 runs bunker first with a two-coach train on the Down line approaching Clegg Street station. No details are known of the origin or destination of the train. Mumps No.1 signal box has stood at this location since being opened in 1885 with its back to the gas works and the bobby's view unrestricted across to Waterloo Sidings box. Near enough to hold a conversation through the windows!

Jim Davenport

A long-distance view of the railway east of Mumps No.1 box, showing the jumble of buildings which formed the townscape of Oldham. Heading from Mumps station is Stanier tank **42285**, photographed on 11 May 1955. The area of ground nearest the camera was originally owned by the Anglo American Oil Company Ltd. which supplied petrol to local businesses. This Company formed an agreement with the LNWR on 9 July 1891 for a private siding, 93 yards long, with subsequent renewals of the agreement up to 1922. The last of these was dated 20 December 1922 after which agreements were made with the LMS. Two readily identifiable features are the Corporation gas holders, and the tower of Oldham Parish Church.

(Above) **The same train** (Opposite page - lower) on the same day is just about to pass under Rhodes Bank footbridge. The bridge, locally known as Gas Street footbridge, was subject to apportionment of maintenance costs between the OA&GB and the L&Y, and later between the OA&GB Joint Board and the LMS. This meant that each had to pay a share of the maintenance cost according to the portion of the bridge over each respective railway. The wrought iron lattice work appears to be blanked off on the Mumps station side; this is because a second bridge ran closely alongside, mounted on concrete piers. This iron girder bridge carried electric cables from Greenhill Electricity Works and was in use by 1 July 1926. It was demolished in July 1985. Both: *Graham Whitehead*

(Right-centre) **Waterloo Sidings signal box** was a difficult subject of photograph in close up without trespassing on the railway. This unusual shot was taken from the pavement along Waterloo Street, almost beneath Bridge 34 which carried the main running lines. Half hidden by the robust stone retaining wall, the box and its adjoining porch peep above the coping stones. This was not an L&Y box but owed its origin to the GCR section of the OA&GB Railway Company. Attractive barge boards and finials adorned the box. Bridge 34A bearing the goods lines over Waterloo Street was demolished in June 1976. *Author's Collection*

(Right-lower) **Fairburn 2-6-4T 42114** runs light engine towards Central station, circa 1960. The loco has just passed over Waterloo Street bridge, the parapet of which can be seen to the left of the coal bunker. Directly opposite is Waterloo Sidings signal box which had, prior to closure, 60 levers (44w 16s) in a RSCo. frame. The box was operated Monday to Friday, from 5 a.m. to 11.30 p.m., and on Saturday, 5 a.m. to 12.15 p.m. Note the line of vans in Waterloo Sidings behind the box. *Ron Amis*

(Left) **Bridge 35 constituted Rhodes Bank footbridge**, seen in this photograph taken in 1994, looking south east towards Glodwick. Today it is regarded as a public thoroughfare between Churchill Street East to a footpath leading back to Mumps station, or across the by-pass to the town centre. The LMS Bridge Register furnished details of the bridge, ranking it as a private bridge and consisting of five spans. For the record, these spans are as follows: over the main lines - 72ft; over goods sidings - 56ft, 47ft, and 31ft. The bridge is a wrought iron lattice girder/floor plate construction and measures 9ft between parapets. There are brick abutments at each end whilst five 1ft diameter cast iron columns support the bridge across the railway. It was constructed in 1880. The photograph is a modern view, of course, showing iron railings inside the lattice work which are an extra safety measure. ***Author***

RHODES BANK "GAS STREET" FOOTBRIDGE

Stanier Class 5 44949 passes under Rhodes Bank footbridge with empty mineral wagons from Higginshaw Gas Works, 15 June 1968. The view shows the degree of dereliction in this part of Oldham, not half a mile from the town centre. In the middle foreground, beyond the brick boundary wall, is the site of the early Rhodes Bank Electricity Works which opened in 1898. All this and more was to be razed to the ground to make way for the by-pass which today skirts the railway at this point. The diagonal stripe on the 16T wagon indicates at which end a door opens for the discharge of contents.

Peter Hutchinson

OA&GB FAREWELL

Push-and-pull fitted Class 13 4-4-2T **67417** leaves Clegg Street station and heads for the Glodwick Road terminus on the last day of service, 2 May 1959. The final train to leave Clegg Street for Stockport was propelled by the same locomotive, leaving Oldham at 10.12 p.m. 67417 carried a headboard on its smokebox door denoting the significance of the day. In the background is the skeletal form of what became Oldham's Parcel Concentration Depot.

Ron Amis

Major re-signalling and trackwork changes took place in the Oldham area between Sunday 7 May and Sunday 21 May 1967. It was on the last of these dates that six signal boxes were closed and replaced by a new box which was to be named simply OLDHAM. Thus, Sheepwashers Lane, Waterloo Sidings, Werneth Station, Mumps Nos. 1, 2 and 3 were closed as from 21 May 1967, their varied operations taken over by the new box located 38 yards on the Rochdale side of the former Waterloo Sidings box. The following series of photographs illustrate the changes as observed by different photographers from Rhodes Bank footbridge.

(Right) On 20 May 1967, Ian Holt's camera captured a Cravens/Rolls Royce torque converter DMU set - based at Accrington - as it heads for Mumps on a Victoria to Rochdale service. Apart from the removal of the Up and Down Lees to Ashton lines, an interesting feature is the presence of Waterloo Sidings and Mumps No.1 boxes with the newcomer, probably on this date, not working - a truly transitional stage in the alterations. The right-hand bracket signal on the down side is unusual; for sighting purposes the Up stop signal arm was mounted on the same bracket as the Down stop and distant arms.

From Rhodes Bank footbridge Jim Davenport took this photograph of a Black Five leaving Clegg Street Sidings with a train of parcel vans on a westbound freight. Close examination reveals that Waterloo Sidings box no longer stands in line with the new box, which, incidentally, was named "Oldham Mumps", and not simply "Oldham" as detailed in Section C notices. Not only has trackwork been substantially altered but the work of re-cabling for track circuiting and motorised pointwork has been underway; the contractors have left the wooden BICC calenders to prove their work at this location.

One evening in July 1967 a thoroughly grimy Black Five, No 45196, draws the 20.30 parcels train out of Clegg Street depot, en route to Carlisle. This journey was probably one of the last the Stanier made before being withdrawn and scrapped. Not only has the original layout at Oldham been slimmed down to the bare minimum, but observers would begin to see the advent of diesel locomotive haulage by the likes of Type 2s and Type 4s. Almost completely hiding the L&NWR curved warehouse is the modern Parcels Concentration Depot, the hopeful answer to the decline of goods handling in the town.

(Left - centre) The subject of this picture by **Jim Davenport** was the scruffy 'Black Five' whose number is unidentifiable due to the coating of filth which has been allowed to build up. Scrawled on the tender side is the enigmatic message *The Blue Jacket Job*. The loco is reversing from Oldham Parcel Concentration Depot (PCD) on an unknown date, possibly in the early 1960s. Beyond the loco are Clegg Street Sidings which curve behind the PCD, on this occasion occupied by a long rake of vans, plus the Woodstock Street end of Clegg Street footbridge. The many-windowed building (top left) is the Star Mill which appears to be in the course of demolition.

(Left - lower) BR Standard 4-6-0 73014 heads away from Mumps with a parcels train on the Up main line towards Werneth, July 1967, barely two months after the extensive remodelling scheme have been completed. Careful observation reveals that balanced bracket signal ahead of this train is without arms as is another left-hand bracket arrangement just beyond Oldham Mumps box. The route via Clegg Street station has been reduced to Up and Down sidings which terminate in the proximity of the former Sheepwashers Lane signal box.   All: *Jim Davenport*

The arrival of Stanier 8F **48476** and BR Standard Class 5 **73069** marks the occasion of the "Farewell to Steam" rail tour at Oldham on 4 August 1968. The tour was run by the RCTS and began at Euston. This was one of the last times that Oldham was treated to a generous coating of sulphurous smoke which can be seen drifting across to Glodwick.

Jim Davenport

(Right - centre) **The new age** - Ex-LMS English Electric 350 hp diesel electric shunter, **12081**, built at Derby Works in November 1950, takes Oldham in its stride. Many drivers, used to the rigours of a loco footplate, found themselves, after training, cocooned in the cab of a diesel locomotive. It was also a new age in health and safety. The eye-catching black and yellow chevron marking on both front and rear of the shunter gave a visual warning to those working nearby. Viewed from Rhodes Bank footbridge on 15 June 1968. *Peter Hutchinson*

(Right - lower) BR Class 25 Sulzer-engined 1,250 hp Bo-Bo diesel electric loco **5210** draws away from Mumps station light engine on 2 July 1971, before working a parcel train out of Clegg Street goods. Forming the background is the industrial blight of Oldham in an area east of Mumps station and Mumps goods yard. The parachute water column standing at the ramp end of the bay platform is a relict feature of the steam era. Observing the filling of tenders and tanks from one of these columns was an experience in itself. The yellow-fronted diesel would have no need for this facility. From Rhodes Bank footbridge this is our first view east towards Mumps station. *Peter Hutchinson*

Crab 2-6-0 No 42733 draws into the western end of Mumps station on an empty stock train bound for Fleetwood during one of the Wakes holidays. Part of the train has still to pass under Rhodes Bank footbridge which is masked in this photograph by the electricity cable bridge. Appearing on the scene (far right) is Mumps No. 2 signal box, housing before closure 21 levers (18w 3s) and open Monday to Sunday from 3.15am to 11.30pm. Note the trap points in the bay line, the purpose of these being to arrest any vehicle passing the bay signal in the on position. *Jim Davenport*

MUMPS No 2

A backward glance from the open window of a train approaching Mumps station, 12 April 1957. There are several features worthy of attention apart from the signal box and its adjoining relay room. The brick building on the other side of the box belongs to the Corporation, as did the ramshackle premises behind it. Entrance to the yard could be made through wooden gates situated behind the box. The buffer stop marks the end of one of the yard's sidings, rail access to which came off the Down Goods Siding and the Down Main by a cross-over. The fogman's pre-cast concrete hut and nearby fire devil completes the railway scene. Leaning against the signal box fuel bunker is the bobby's bicycle, suggesting, perhaps, that he had not travelled far to reach his workplace. *H C Casserley*

A delightful view of Mumps looking towards the bridge which carries the railway over the street known as Mumps. Although a street scene, there are two indications of the nearness of a railway: the bracketed signal with lower-quadrant arms (positioned on the Shaw side of the bridge), and the L&Y station sign affixed to the building at the corner of Coronation Street. The year is thought to be just after the Great War and illustrates that Mumps was a thriving commercial area, thronged with people during the day. An electric tram, bound for Shaw (Wren's Nest) passes over the junction between Yorkshire Street and Union Street, while a lone shire horse plods up hill towards Union Street with an immense load of cotton bales. Clogs, shawls, cloth caps and bowlers, the clomp of horses hooves, and the whine of trams all added to the atmosphere that was Mumps. *Author's Collection*

OLDHAM'S THREE MAIN STATIONS

"Oldham became not only the main centre of cotton spinning in Lancashire but also the leading mill town of the world". This comment made by M Williams and D Farnie (Cotton Mills in Greater Manchester, 1992) firmly attributes the town on a hill with the greatest industrial commercial status in the cotton textile business. No wonder that the aspirations of three railway companies strove in turn to reach for the town and tap the high volume of trade: coal and raw cotton coming in; finished goods in the form of cotton and associated textile machinery going out. The end result led to an extensive railway infrastructure by the turn of the century, one which continued to exist until decline set in during the 1950s.

Of the three principal passenger stations, Mumps has always been regarded as the town's premier station - it has certainly outlived the other two. A major change in the station took place

when the LYR decided to rebuild it in 1884, the contract for the work being let to Thomas Wrigley, work which included the widening of the line for £19,517, during the summer of that year. The new station was reported to be completed in March 1887 and assumed the form of a wide island platform on which the station buildings were mounted, a large overall roof protecting all. Two bays were provided, one at each end of the platform, these being designated the Manchester Bay (at the western end) and the Rochdale Bay, at the other. The station could be approached along Coronation Street and Victoria Street (streets which are now long gone) with a subway and stairs affording access to the platform.

Further improvements took place near the station with the reconstruction of Lees Road Bridge. Board Minutes dated 12 June 1890 refer to the work involved: *"Lees Road bridge to be reconstructed at a cost of £5,717. 17s 4d by the contractors*

A bleak scene in winter at Mumps No. 2 box. This was the prospect encountered on winter mornings as the early turn began at 3.15am. The bobby's outlook with the coming of daylight stretched across the station platforms and beyond to the goods yard. The rear of the box afforded little interest, backing as it did on to the Corporation yard. The dark satanic mill in the misty background is Mumps Mill.   ***Author's Collection***

Holme & King". The outcome of this work resulted in a wrought iron cross-girder and plate structure, with white glazed bricks forming the abutments. It stands today as a reminder of the LYR's presence in the town, and has assumed the sobriquet *"Mumps Bridge"*, where once, two centuries ago, a simple bridge carried a dirt road over Mumps Brook.

The essential character of the station remained until 1925 when its was reported that it was to receive a facelift. The Oldham Weekly Chronicle, 25 January 1975, alludes to the facelift by drawing on the news of fifty years ago. *"Alterations are taking place at Mumps station, Oldham, prior to the introduction of electric trains. The general waiting room has been demolished so as to lengthen the bay at the Manchester end, while the steps on to the platform are to be done away with and passengers will use the slope from the subway. A new ticket collector's cabin has been erected at the top of the slope, and a new waiting room is to be erected over the present steps"*. The allusion to electrification indicates that in 1925 the prospect of electric trains running between Manchester and Rochdale was quite real.

The 1925 improvement is what most people saw as they journeyed to work each day, or patiently waited for the Saturday morning excursion to a favourite holiday resort. Not everyone had pleasant experiences of Oldham's stations, nor of the journey to Manchester from Oldham. The Oldham Chronicle, 21 February 1953, printed a letter which purported to have been written by a

passenger. The letter was published in full, and was accompanied by photographs which depicted the deplorable condition of Oldham's stations in Coronation Year. The letter read thus: *"Arriving at Mumps Station from Mumps Bridge I followed the notice saying 'Booking Office' and was brought up short against a large permanently-locked door. I prowled around the end of the building, but all the entrances were made up. I passed along a line of what seemed to be broken-down wooden partitioning, and eventually found a way in at the further end"*. The letter writer was told by station staff that the locked door had been closed since the war, meaning that for ten years at least the sign to the Booking Office had been directing passengers "to a locked door"; no-one at the station had corrected the situation.

The writer's observations as he travelled through Central and Werneth station were equally condemnatory: *"At Central Station, there was broken masonry rubble and old iron piled high on both platforms in firmly settled piles that looked as if they had been there for weeks if not months. At Werneth, the whole station seemed to covered in layers of peeling filthy paint. I seemed to recognise the paint-work, perhaps because it is the final vestiges of what I used to see fifteen and twenty years ago"*.

British Railways announced in February 1953 that Mumps station was to be rebuilt as a modern structure, finally sweeping away years of neglect and dilapidation. Unlike other local stations Mumps failed to receive a *"Coronation Year"* coat of paint in view of the pending rebuilding programme. After two years of inaction, the Oldham Chronicle, 26 November 1954, lamented the situation referring to *"the station's desolate precincts"*: *"The minor wilderness of hopeless grass, drooping trees, decaying fences, and uneven cobbles fronting Mumps does not lend itself to a vision of an attractive entrance"*. However, BR announced that its was to reconstruct the station in the *Spring* of 1955. Bucked up by this promise of better things, the newspaper that *"The new station is to have a steel frame with steel roof decking. The street frontage will be of brick with extra large windows in the ticket hall, ticket office, and parcels office. Electric lighting will be installed throughout"*. What a difference that alone would have made!

The design of the new station was by J Taylor Thompson, the Chief Civil Engineer of BR (LMR), and the work carried out by Gerrards of Swindon at a cost of £30,000. The station opened on 3 August 1957.

Oldham's goods facilities reflected the town's industrial standing. At Mumps, three large goods sheds lay to the south east of the station, both L&Y and LNWR premises, with ample siding accommodation serving them. One LNWR brick-built shed still stands with its wall facing the Royal Mail Sorting Office along Hamilton Street, utilised by two fork-lift truck enterprises (1999).

At the other end of town were Central and Clegg Street stations, not unique in themselves but in their contiguity. The 1861 OS map shows the underdeveloped LYR Central station sited on the western side of Clegg Street Bridge. The station was opened on 1 November 1847. A new station was developed on the same site between 1864 and 1866, the following LYR Board Minutes summarising its evolution: *6 July 1864.* John Thompson, of Cheetham Hill, offers tender of £5,356. This was accepted by the LYR Board. In May 1864, Sturges Meek, the LYR chief engi-

A view from the open window of the 12.05pm Victoria to Royton train arriving at the down main line at Mumps, 12 April 1957. The station is a scene of activity with the bunker end of a tank engine and its train awaiting departure in the bay, and an Aspinall "A" Class 0-6-0 coming through the station from the direction of Royton. Right of centre it is just possible to make out the lattice footbridge spanning the Oldham Branch between the LNWR goods warehouse and Hamilton Street. The bridge was No. 28 on the Branch, the numbering reading from Greenfield Junction. The LNWR double-bay, three-storey warehouse had three enclosed hoists separated by three awnings over loading platforms; it was similar to the one at Clegg Street Goods, but a rectilinear version. Few photographs of Oldham fail to show a cotton mill at some location. In this case, Greenbank Mills and associated chimney make an appearance.

H C Casserley

neer had estimated the cost of the new station at £8,000. *15 August 1866.* Total cost of completed station £7,587.

The final form of the station after 1880 possessed two platforms, served by the up and down through lines. Beneath the glazed canopies there was ample provision for passengers' needs - down platform urinals, Gents' Waiting Room, General Waiting Room, Ladies First and Third Class Waiting Room (with WCs), Station Master's Office, Parcels Office, and Porters' Room. The up side had the same provision, minus the latter three, the space left being made up of a Telegraph Office and Booking Office. A footbridge linked the Booking Office with the down platform, via a set of stairs.

Clegg Street station lay on either side of Clegg Street, one of the principal streets which extended south from the town centre. The northernmost extremity of the OAGB line curved its way through Sheepwashes Lane Tunnel, through the station, to unite with the LYR line at Oldham Junction (known in railway parlance as Rubber Junction). Clegg Street was the larger of the

two stations, opening on 26 August 1861. The first station stood east of Clegg Street Bridge with platforms extending towards Mumps. The space between Clegg Street Bridge and the tunnel portal was too short for the platforms to extend the other way. An overall roof covered the station area, with the Booking Office facing on to Clegg Street.

The OS plan of 1879 reveals that the distance between Clegg Street Bridge and Sheepwashes Tunnel had been increased so allowing the station to develop southwards and resulting in a lengthy down platform, a short up platform with a single-road bay. An additional feature was a loop line which circumvented the down platform so making it an island platform, and separating it from the adjoining Central station. Reference to the evolution of the station was made in the Oldham Chronicle, 1 January 1921, on the retirement of Joseph Young, a railway employee at the station for fifty years. The following account reflects the changes which were observed by Mr Young during his years of service: *"In 1875, a loop line as made at Clegg Street, that eking out the former*

Major changes have occurred at Mumps station so that by April 1957, when this photograph was taken, renewal and modernisation set the scene. The "new" station was opened on 6 September in that year; the view is from the up side of the bay platform. New electric lamp standards have been installed, plus new BR(LMR) steel plate station signs - white lettering on a maroon background. Work on the station is still in progress: an electrician works on the wiring at the base of a lamp, shielded from the wind by a sheet draped round a set of step ladders. One of the original lamps proudly stands as a reminder of gaslight days. *H C Casserley*

From aboard a train which has come off the Oldham Branch and heading for Clegg Street station, the photorapher took a backward glance at Mumps No. 2 signal box and Mumps station. This 19 April 1954 photograph affords a view of the signal box before it received remedial attention. Mumps station looks as though it too needs attention to the roof, the ends of which are missing leaving the sub-structure exposed. It was not until August 1957, however, that the station received overdue refurbishment. Mumps Mill dominates the scene, but was demolished in 1969 after lying idle for seventeen years. *H C Casserley*

text continued..........Down and Up line and enabling traffic to be dealt with better. But with the improvement there was a contretemps: the funnel of the first engine through the loop was knocked off by the bridge. The easiest way to put matters right and prevent any similar mishap was to lower the level of the line, and this was done.... Within the past 20 years, Clegg Street station has been largely rebuilt [actually rebuilt between 1899 and 1901], and made more comfortable, this work taking some 2 1/2 years. Formerly there were no waiting rooms on the Up platform, and the improvement that was made on that side was especially welcome, for to wait for a Greenfield train on a windy night at the old station was a very disagreeable experience. Electric lighting at the station [and at the goods yard] are also among the changes that have been wrought from the conditions of the '70s".

An LMS rating plan shows the final disposition of the station which remained until its closure on 4 May 1959. A generous provision of passenger accommodation appears on both platforms including a refreshment room on the Up platform, the only such provision at any of Oldham's stations, although this is not shown on the plan. Nor does the plan show the milk hoist (located at the southern part of the down platform) and the bridge which allowed the dispatch of milk churns from the island platform to the adjacent goods yard. This facility was removed in 1940. The closure of the station in 1959 gave Clegg Street station the dubious merit of being the first station to close in the town. The last train to leave Clegg Street was the 10.12 pm Oldham to Stockport, hauled by LNER Class C13, No. 67417 (a regular on the OAGB line), emphasising the point by boasting a headboard on the smokebox door which read *"Old Ashton and Guide Bridge Railway Last Day May 2"*. ....*continued on page 66*

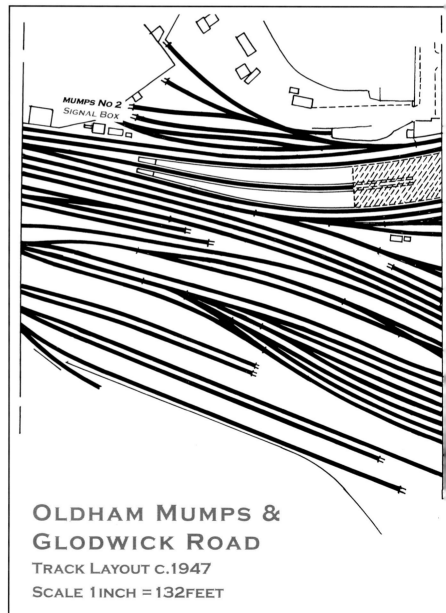

MUMPS No 2
SIGNAL BOX

OLDHAM MUMPS & GLODWICK ROAD

TRACK LAYOUT C.1947

SCALE 1 INCH = 132 FEET

This photograph can be compared with the one (Opposite) for 1954, this time taken from a train leaving Mumps station on the up main line. Mumps No. 2 box has now benefited from a lick of paint, and the station roof has been attended to. The new lift shaft housing peeps above the van stabled in the siding.

H C Casserley

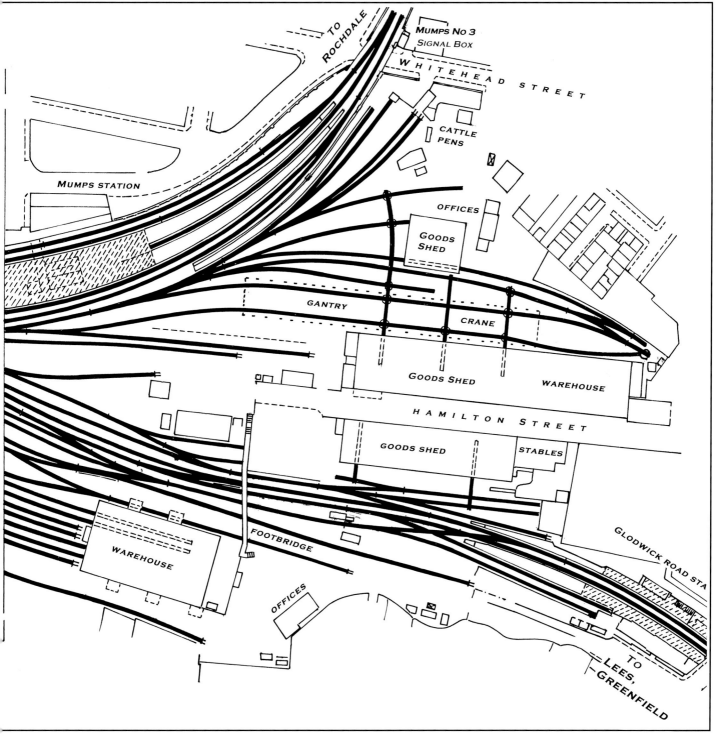

MUMPS STATION

TO ROCHDALE

MUMPS No 3 SIGNAL BOX

WHITEHEAD STREET

CATTLE PENS

OFFICES

GOODS SHED

GANTRY

CRANE

GOODS SHED

WAREHOUSE

HAMILTON STREET

GOODS SHED

STABLES

FOOTBRIDGE

WAREHOUSE

OFFICES

GLODWICK ROAD STA

TO LEES, GREENFIELD

The last days of the old station building, photographed on a sunny day in early Spring, 6 March 1956. As well as providing a record of the building, the photograph also illustrates how unattractive the frontage is. Seen here, the building is closed to the public, presumably while contractors remove the interior fittings pending demolition. Meanwhile, as a reminder of how bad things are, broken windows, missing panes, and shabby woodwork face the traveller, not to mention the missing section of awning, and the makeshift shelter at the far end. All in all, a forlorn spectacle. A notice board directs the public to a timber hut from which tickets can be bought. It is not clear, however, how access to and exit from the platform could be made while this temporary measure was in existence.   *BR(LMR)*

Despite the 1957 reconstruction much remained recognisable of ex-L&Y structures and fittings which gave the station its down-at-heel character. Once through the new building, 1957 was left behind; it was like stepping back into a by-gone age albeit enhanced by electric lights. The following photographs (dated 19 August 1975) depict this retrospective vision.   *BR(LMR)*

(Right - centre) The subway: this was faced with light - reflecting brickwork, the sides of which are protected by wooden barriers against the impact of trolleys. Overhead, rivetted wrought iron beams carry the down lines whilst lattice girders bear the weight of the platform. Steps at the far end have to be ascended in order to reach the exit. At the foot of the steps, on the left, is the opening to the goods hoist.

(Right - lower) Leaving the subway leads the passenger to the first section of the inclined approach to the platform. White-glazed and patterned brickwork continues from the subway, with hand rail (for pedestrians on that side) and trolley barrier opposite. Daylight beckons at platform level, and an electric light shows that someone is present in the porters room.

There is much in the photograph which reveals the legacy of the L&Y. It shows the incline rising up from the subway to the down platform side of the island platform. The wrought iron railings and the cast iron standards into which they are fitted, the ornate brickwork and the wooden panelling around the windows all owe their origin to the 'Business Line'. Many a foot-weary person has trudged up this slope, and many shift-weary railwaymen have plodded homewards along it. The poster on the wall announces that YOU CAN'T RENT MORE UP-TO-DATE SETS OR BETTER SERVICE - MULTI BROADCAST. 19 inch TV sets were offered for rental at 7/9 (39p) from a retailer in town. *Eric Blakey LYRS Collection*

(Right - centre) Never missing a detail, Eric paused at the goods hoist at the end of the subway to photograph the L&Y cast iron plate affixed to the wall above the hoist gates. The notice reads: GOODS HOIST ONLY. NOT TO BE USED BY PASSENGERS AND UNAUTHORISED PERSONS. TABLE TO BE LEFT WITH SUBWAY. BEFORE MOVING HOIST OPERATOR MUST SEE THAT NO ONE AT THE OTHER LEVEL IS ABOUT TO USE IT. THE GATES MUST NOT BE LEANED AGAINST. BY ORDER. *Eric Blakey LYRS Collection*

(Below) Only BR station signs detract from the L&Y ambience, even in the mid-seventies. The door to the Waiting Room faces us in this view, a door with a brass knob turned by many thousands over the years. The square timber hut served as the ticket collector's refuge - a welcome shelter from winter draughts and rail-laden air while tickets are inspected and punched. The WAY OUT sign directs the public to a set of stairs behind the waiting room which descend to the subway.

Mumps station was again the focus of interest in this photograph taken on 19 August 1975 from the grassy reservation of the town by - pass. Various changes have occurred since the £30,000 reconstruction of 1957. Victoria Street, which formed the setted approach has been replaced by a tarmac fore-court which opens on to the by-pass. New fluorescent lighting has also been erected to effect good lighting in an important thoroughfare for traffic and pedestrians. This end of the building possesses the hoist which is housed in the rectangular block, with a slide shutter door at street level. Behind, we can see the partially glazed platform roof peeping above the modern building.

BR(LMR)

*Continued from page 62........*Central station followed suit on 18 April 1966. Nothing is left, save for a fragment of carved stonework which once graced the Down platform - this can be fleetingly seen as a reminder of what was as trains pass the site of the station today. Central station's demise was acknowledged in the Oldham Chronicle, 17 January 1966, under the headline pun *"End of the Line for Central Station"*. *"Just as the flickering gas lamps fail to dispel the gloomy atmosphere, so the station, which once echoed with the clatter of clogs, is too old and tired to adapt itself to the needs of modern travel"*.

　　　Between Woodstock Street and the stations lay Clegg Street Goods Depot. The origin of the depot reaches back to the formative years of the 1860s, end even before then. Certainly by 1879 there were two goods sheds (one LNWR owned, the other

MS&LR) which stood on either side of Sheepwashes Lane Tunnel. By this time, a long lattice footbridge extended from Woodstock Street to Clegg Street, over the curved sidings of the depot. The 1894 OS plan shows the full maturity of the depot, with all the sidings completed, and a third goods shed in preparation. The only reminder of the one-time busy depot is the forlorn and neglected LNWR warehouse, standing close to Park Road, a listed building and a town planner's nightmare.

　　　The depot found a new lease of life in the early 1960s with the commissioning of the Parcel Concentration Depot which began functioning in 1960. As early as 1953 the Burlington Mail Order Company opened at the Earl Mill, Downy Street, from which parcels were taken to Clegg Street goods for rail distribution. It was not until the beginning of the new decade that the vol

.....................*continued opposite*

The Manchester bay end of the platform shows the stop-block surrounded on three sides by a timber shield. Far to the right is the abandoned goods yard, and to the left the brick wall of the station building. In August 1975 the Up Through Goods line is still in place, but the Down Through Goods line has been taken out.

BR(LMR)

One of the earliest post-war photographs of Mumps station is this example, taken on 20 April 1953. The view shows the down platform (for trains to Royton, Shaw, and Rochdale) as more or less built by the L&Y in 1887. Beneath the roof over the island platform are the platform buildings, the one nearest the camera being the Gents. A variety of furniture includes the parcel trolleys, seats (cast iron frame, wooden seat and backrest), and a set of mobile step ladders for reaching those high places. Arrangements are in hand to re-surface some part of the station - note the concrete paving leaning against the wall. Of interest are the advertisement posters: the nearest - Totectors - your guarantee of safety (these were heavy-duty boots with steel toe caps) .Other posters concern the B&L Line from Liverpool to Dublin;.....................*continued below*

ume of traffic merited the construction of a new parcel depot. Other mail order companies in Oldham operated through the depot so that in 1961 some 45,000 parcels were being handled daily. As the largest depot of its kind in the North West it was, by 1977, making an annual loss of £800,000, brought about probably by the mail order business preference for road transport. The depot was disbanded with the loss of 200 jobs in October 1980, leaving a 30 acre site to await re-development.

Even further west, at Werneth, goods facilities were provided on the south side of the station from an early date, complete with two small goods sheds. This was soon found to be inadequate and more sidings were laid in an area to the north of the station, bounded on the west by Featherstall Road South, and on the east by a stone retaining wall which curved back from the portal of Werneth Tunnel. The 1879 OS plan shows that a goods shed had been erected parallel to Featherstall Road South; LYR Board Minutes indicated that Messrs Wade's tender of £9,550 was accepted for the work

on 17 January 1872. Access to the goods yard by road could be made from Featherstall Road South.

With expanding trade, these sidings too were deemed overstretched and by purchasing land to the north of West Street, the LYR laid out further sidings between 1886 and 1888. Thomas Wrigley's tender of £18,359 was accepted for a weigh office, boundary wall, entrance gate, warehouse and shed on 21 December 1886. He also won the contract for paving the yard with Haslingden setts at a cost of 4s 2d per square yard, the contract for this dated 22 February 1888. A travelling overhead crane which had worked in the lower sidings was removed along with the goods shed, the former being erected on the eastern side of the new sidings. Werneth Goods station eventually possessed a large cotton shed built under contract by S Warburton for a tender price of £9,715.4s 3d, accepted by the LYR Board on 26 September 1901. Access to Werneth Goods station could be had from Middleton Road.

.... the delights of Northern Ireland, Essex, and shopping. At the top of each are the words London, Midland & Scottish, or simply LMS. The Gentlemen sign is pure L&Y.

(Right - lower) In later L&Y days, this Benn & Cronin departure board informed the intending traveller inside Mumps booking hall. An exit to Victoria Street could be made through the doors marking "Booking and Parcels Offices". The handrail of the stairs leading to the subway appears to the left of the departure board. For the delectation of passengers, a few pennies in one or other of the slot machines would provide Nestle's milk chocolate bars or sweet meat (sugared confectionery), if preferred. And for the man intent on decorating his home or office, the advertisement extols the virtues of using PARIPAN ENAMEL for all painting.   *Author's Collection*

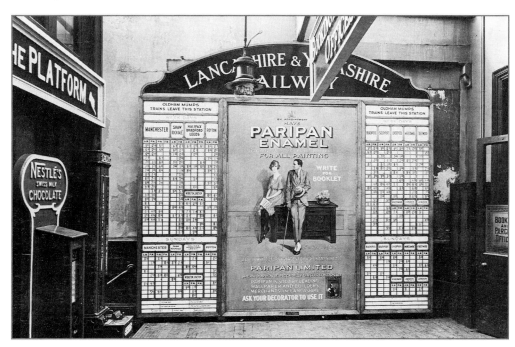

The origins of the Wakes are rooted in antiquity. They were originally a pagan ceremony of harvest thanksgiving held at the beginning of August. During the last decades of the 19th Century Oldham Wakes was allocated to the last Saturday in August, a situation which lasted until 1947, with two exceptions. In 1879 the date of the Wakes was moved to the first Saturday in August, and this became known as the *"School Board Wakes"*. It was kept in 1879, 1880 and 1881. After the 1881 Wakes, the holiday reverted to the end of the month, but in 1919 and 1920 the holiday was positioned at the second week of June at the request of the railway companies. The reason for this is uncertain but may have something to do with the fact that Rochdale Wakes was held at the same time, and this created operational problems for the L&Y.

Workers were encouraged to save for their Wakes holiday by allocating a proportion of their wages each week to a holiday fund. In the early 1950s, such clubs included factories and mills, Sunday schools, day schools, public houses, breweries and social clubs. In 1950, for instance, the biggest pay-out was attributed to Ferranti Ltd with a total of £47,500, seconded by Platt Bros. at £39,000. In the same year, Wakes savings club funds totalled £600,000, or if averaged out, £9,560 per club.

It was reported in the Oldham Chronicle, 16 June 1950, on the eve of the Wakes (the Wakes in 1950 began on Saturday, 17 June) that *'A further weight of passenger traffic will be taken over the weekend by British Railways who are running about fifty trains on excursions out of town. Bookings for these were reported as 'not bad at all'* The weather broke as the holiday began, following a heat-wave.

In 1951 it was plain that competition faced British Railways. Two coaching companies advertised in the press in a *"Joint Annual Holiday Excursion Programme"* with bookings being taken from 11 June. The joint programme was instigated by *Holts of Oldham Ltd* and *Yelloway Motor Services Ltd.* Holts ran coaches from their offices at Mumps to Carnarvon, Stratford upon Avon, New Brighton, Morecambe, Scarborough, Harrogate and Knaresborough, Bettws-y-Coed, Southport, Bridlington, and Chester. Yelloway had a regular daily service of four coaches to Blackpool from Oldham and Shaw. I have vague memories of standing with my parents at the site of Bradley Bent Basin, Hollinwood, near the Roxy Cinema, awaiting a coach to transport us to some now forgotten destination. The filled in basin originally formed the terminus of the Hollinwood Branch of the Manchester, Ashton-under-Lyne Canal, and in the 1950s was the starting-point for some coach operators.

The Oldham Chronicle, 22 June 1951, hinted that the Wakes railway traffic might be curtailed owing to an apparent shortage of engines and crews to runs them. When all seemed hopeless, it was announced that *"British Railways, who it was thought might have to cut holiday specials because of accumulated freight traffic, have maintained a full programme of about fifty trains for excursions. Holidaymakers will probably start arriving at Mumps Station as early as 6 a.m. tomorrow".*

The possible threat, real or imagined, was something that BR could readily do without, bearing in mind the competition from coach operators. The 1951 Wakes period passed without any serious difficulty, and holidaymakers were keen to send back to Oldham thousands of postcards. On Monday, 25th and Tuesday, 26th June the following number of cards were counted which gives some idea of the destinations at this time: Blackpool - 14,000;

North Wales - 11,000; Isle of Man - 7,500; Morecambe - 7,300; South Coast - 6,100; East Coast - 5,600; Fleetwood and Southport - 5,000; New Brighton - 2,350; continental - 2,500. Not of all of these, of course, had reached their destinations by rail.

The Oldham Chronicle, 15 June 1955, carried a public announcement three days before the Wakes began. Much to the relief of thousands of Oldhamers, special holiday trains were made available by BR despite a two-week A.S.L.E.F. strike which was settled a few days before. The planned arrangements were reported in the Chronicle as follows:

Friday 17 June
8 pm   Mumps to Heysham.
8.36 pm Mumps to Torquay, Paignton and Cornwall.
        (Both of these trains picked up passengers at Central Station, Werneth, Hollinwood, and Failsworth).
9 pm   Clegg Street to Newquay.
9.26pm Mumps to Bath, Poole, and Bournemouth.
9.40pm Mumps to Fleetwood (for Isle of Man).
10.5pm Mumps to Norwich and Great Yarmouth.
10.45pm Mumps to Brighton, Hastings, and Eastbourne.
11.10pm Mumps to Portsmouth (for Isle of Wight).
11.35pm Mumps to Holyhead (for Eire).
11.46pm Mumps to Glasgow *(picking up at Central, Werneth, Hollinwood, and Failsworth).*

Friday night/Saturday morning
10.25pm Greenfield to West of England,
        calling at Clegg Street at 10.42pm
12.13am Greenfield to Euston,
        calling at Clegg Street at 12.30am
7.34am Mumps to Liverpool (for steamer to Llandudno and Menai Bridge).
8.40am Greenfield to Norwich and Great Yarmouth,
        calling at Clegg Street at 8.55am
10.14am Greenfield to North Wales,
        calling at Clegg Street at 10.26am

In addition to these specials, there was a normal service to Blackpool, Fleetwood, Southport, Lancaster and Morecambe, the Lake District, North Wales, Bridlington, Filey, Scarborough, and Skegness.

Not all of these trains, specials or otherwise, were fully taken or required, a point which the Oldham Chronicle, 18 June 1955, commented upon: *"A train to Fleetwood was cancelled because of the small demand for seats. This, it is thought, was due to the price of the tickets - 18s 6d - compared with only 10s 6d to Blackpool, although there are only a few miles difference in the two journeys".*

In 1956, the *"Oldham and District Holidays"* were acknowledged in the Chronicle of 23 June, under the banner headline *"Grand Send-Off to £1M Wakes Rush".* The newspaper commented that *"Special trains left for the South Coast last night and Mumps station handled traffic until 1am this morning. But by 5am the station began to fill again with people travelling to destinations in Wales and on the Lancashire and Yorkshire coasts. An official said that by 10.30am the station was beginning to resume normal routine, having handled thousands of holidaymakers".*

Before the last war, Oldham annual holidays - the Wakes week - commenced at the end of August. In 1938, for example, the holiday began on Friday, 26 August, most workers leaving factories, mills, shops, and offices to make last - minute preparations or to travel on the Friday evening. In this photograph, it is not known whether the crowd standing on Mumps Up side platform is travelling on the Friday or the Saturday. But the long wait is over as an unidentified 'Black Five' eases into the station displaying the reporting number W442A. One noticeable absent feature is a check rail on the inner rail nearest the platform wall. *Oldham Evening Chronicle*

There was a wet start to the Wakes in June 1953. A small gathering of cheerful people stands on Mumps station in anticipation of the arrival of the train to Blackpool. This photograph appeared in the Oldham Evening Chronicle a few days later where it was commented that despite the new opportunities for holiday travel, Blackpool still attracted many holidaymakers. The photograph was taken just as a tank engine draws into the station, bunker first. *Oldham Evening Chronicle*

An excursion with a difference. A troop of boy scouts awaits the train on the Rochdale side of the station, probably at the start of a week's camping trip in 1957. The station was extensively refurbished in 1957 although there are few signs of this in the photograph. The roof sub-structure and the former L&Y platform buildings remain undisturbed, whilst the absence of litter is significant. The station was manned at this time and under the watchful eye of the station master so that any untidiness was quickly dealt with so keeping the station spick and span. *Oldham Evening Chronicle*

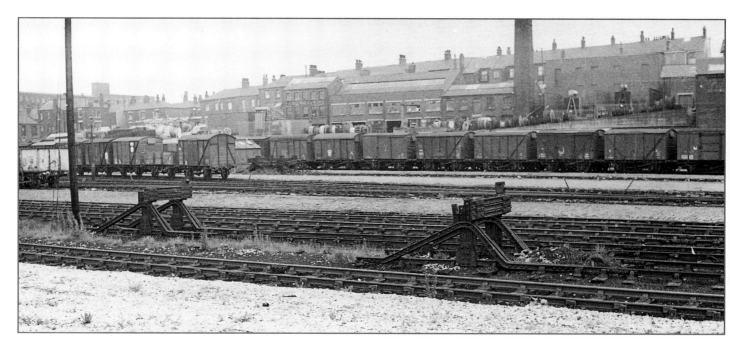

Oldham Mumps goods sidings (or part of them) were photographed from the Werneth end of the station on 25 June 1966. The urban backcloth is made of Greenhill Electricity Works and other industrial premises, plus rows of terraced houses lying in the shadow of a cotton mill in the left distance. The electricity works was reverently known as *"The Old Faithful"* and had opened on 15 June 1903 to replace the small and inadequate Rhodes Bank Electricity Works. Not much of the Greenhill Works can be observed but close inspection reveals the oil reservoirs for the transformers in the adjacent yard. Lack of coal during the 1926 General Strike led to a temporary conversion to oil burning, but re-conversion took place when coal supplies returned to normal. The works was still in operation in February 1954, soon to be eclipsed by Chadderton Power Station. The number of vans in the yard reflects the importance of Oldham's Parcels Concentration Depot.

Eric Blakey LYRS Collection

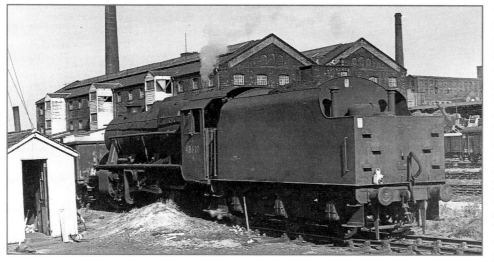

This could have been a superb study of the ex-LNWR goods warehouse were it not for the Stanier 8F intruding onto the scene. Jim Davenport evidently thought that the locomotive was worth recording for posterity and is the main focus of interest. In 1966 the warehouse had long been designated LONDON MIDLAND AND SCOTTISH WAREHOUSE and this is proclaimed on the wall facing the station. LNWR Minutes, dated 19 October 1887, record that the tender of W A Peters & Son, contractors of Rochdale, was accepted at £17,010 for warehouse and stables. A goods warehouse occupying the same site and measuring 266ft x 75ft is shown on a LNWR plan of December 1884. This was possibly demolished and replaced by the 1887 construction, complete with three hoists and four internal cranes. Two pairs of lines entered the warehouse and terminated at stop blocks at a wide loading deck.

In remarkably presentable condition, Ivatt Class 2MT **46523** pauses for Jim Davenport's photographic attention, circa 1960. The locomotive was a product built to satisfy LMSR requirements in the early post-war years. H G Ivatt designed two types for secondary services, one of them being the 2-6-0, the other the 2-6-2 tank version. One 128 of these tender engines were manufactured, incorporating modern details such as rocking grates and self-emptying ash pans, along with other refinements.

THE MUMPS 'PILOTS'

(Right - upper and centre) The old order of things is represented by two ex-L&Y Aspinall 0-6-0 workhorses, Nos. **52248** and **52486.** Each is standing waiting for action at Mumps Goods Yard, circa 1959/60. These engines would spend their time on shunting duties with occasional trip working to deliver or collect wagons at near-by yards. 52248, a Lees engine, was built at Horwich and placed into traffic on 7 September 1894; it was withdrawn in March 1962. 52486, another Lees engine, was also built at Horwich, and began its working life on 31 October 1918; it was withdrawn in October 1960.

LANKY VETERANS

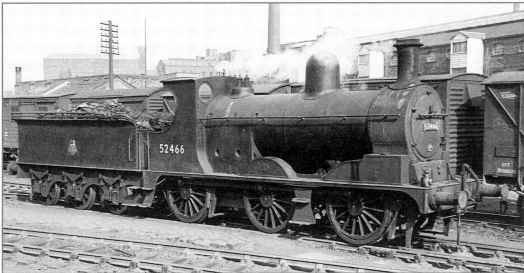

(Right - lower) Old and new at Mumps, June 1966. On a sunny summer day, Jim Davenport caught both on camera from the safety of the western end of the up platform. We have already seen in a previous picture, **48620** standing alongside the ash mound. Here she is again with signs of activity in the shape of a BR 350 hp diesel shunter, **12081**, the forerunner of the ubiquitous Class 08 shunting loco. 12081 was withdrawn in 1970 and cut up at C F Booth, Rotherham. One-man operated, the driver (complete with traditional grease cap) peers from his cab whilst the shunter, with traditional pole, looks across to the platform. The high visibility striped front (and rear) of the diesel contrasts with total absence of safety wear the man with the pole.

All: *Jim Davenport*

A winter scene at Mumps Goods Yard. No date is indicated when this photograph was taken, but the lack of activity about the yard suggests a Saturday afternoon or Sunday, circa 1960. Formerly the L&Y goods yard, the most noticeable feature is the travelling crane which was employed in transferring loads from road to rail (and vice versa). The first mention of a steam travelling crane appeared in the Manchester Guardian on 25 March 1872 in a contract advertisement. The one shown here was a version operated by electricity. Turning up on a bitterly cold Monday morning before daybreak, to spend an eight hour day as a shunter, crane driver, or yard man, must have been thoroughly demoralising. *Jim Davenport*

Stanier 8F 48745 is working a trip freight on the Up Goods line, circa 1960. The first two wagons are recognisable as Conflats which were used for conveying A-type containers employed in BR's Freightliner service. The Up Goods line was taken out of use on 14 May 1967 and retained as a siding terminating at a stop block 100 yards on the station side of Mumps No. 3 box. As such, it was renamed "Siding". Far to the right there is a glimpse of the overhead travelling crane in Mumps Goods Yard. *Jim Davenport*

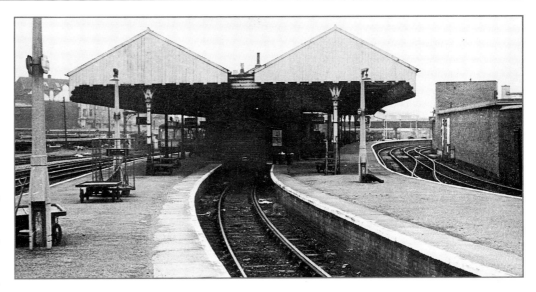

Views taken at the Rochdale end of the station are uncommon, photographers preferring to stand at the western end. From the edge of the down platform Eric Blakey has captured a scene which embraces the old and the new - the roof over the platform, and the 1957 brick station building. Compared to the exterior which met the public in the early 1950s, the new building was an improvement. Even the tree and grass open space lent a measure of relief in a heavily built up area. The brick wall with chamfered buttresses was later raised to the same height of the wall coping at the far end. Note the check rail on the down main line and the trap point to arrest the progress of goods trains in the event of failing to stop at an on signal.

(Right - centre) Another viewpoint from the Rochdale end of the station. The up platform curved continuously throughout its length whilst the down platform, also curved, has one straight section roughly midway. Facing on to the straight section is the rear wall of the 1957 building, the highest part of which is the hoist. The latter enabled parcels, etc, to be lifted from the subway to street level - a useful facility where working levels are different. Pausing to pick up passengers on the up side is a Manchester - bound DMU which has arrived from Rochdale. The Rochdale bay was taken out of use on 14 May 1967 and subsequently filled in so this end of the island platform became inordinately wide.

(Right - lower) The view from the Rochdale end of the platform on 25 June 1966. Working its way towards the station past No. 3 box is 'Black Five' No **44827** with a goods train. The signal box at this time accommodated 25 levers (21w 4s). It was manned Monday to Saturday from 4am to 11.30pm or later if Manchester Control gave alternative instructions. The view from the end windows of the box overlooked Whitehead Street, a street which was soon to disappear in the redevelopment of the Mumps area. The inveterate features we see here were to be changed completely over two years later.

*All: **Eric Blakey** LYRS Collection*

The disposition of the roads, streets, and buildings east of Mumps station has been a problem for many years. The Oldham Chronicle, 27 February 1892, reported that The congestion of traffic at the old bridge was a matter of daily occurrence and it was recognised that a much-needed improvement had been brought about by the construction of a new bridge. The new bridge consisted of two wrought iron plate girders, 103ft and 107ft long, and 11ft deep, weighing 52 and 56 tons respectively. The weight of the floor carrying the railway was 80 tons. The construction was undertaken by the Liverpool firm of Holme & King as a joint improvement scheme between the L&Y and Oldham Corporation, costing £20,647 3s 4d. Bridge 25 currently spans the northern side of Mumps Roundabout. Bridge 24 spanned Whitehead Street a short distance from the station. In 1892 Whitehead Street was described as a thoroughfare which passes beneath the L&Y Railway lines…. and was no more than a way for foot passengers only. It had been an arch only 16ft wide with a headroom of 9ft 6ins. An earlier rebuilding scheme of 1886 reconstructed Bridge 24 so that the street was widened to 36ft and the headroom increased to 14ft.

Proposals to construct the town by-pass were made as early as 1948 but it was not until 1960 that definite plans were made for a four-lane road to carry the increasing volume of traffic from one side of the town to the other. At the Mumps end, major changes were made in the re-shaping of the area closest to the bridges. Streets and property were cleared. Lees Road was re-aligned so that its junction with the roundabout followed the course of Whitehead Street, whilst Bottom o' th' Moor continued to pass beneath Bridge 25. The by-pass was opened on 6 October 1970. The next few photographs depict the re-construction work in progress on Bridge 24.

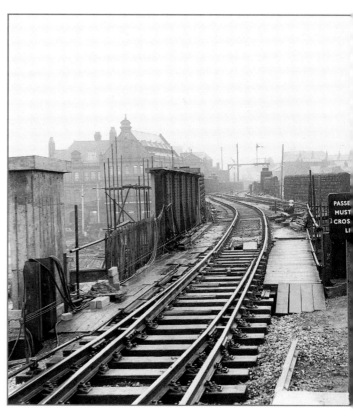

(Above) A view of the proceedings at Bridge 24 taken from the ramp end of the island platform. The 1886 girders are still in place as are the abutments supporting the railway whilst work is going on around them. The normal passage of trains was unaffected during this stage of the rebuilding programme. The upward gradient of 1 in 231 is evident in this view looking towards Royton Junction.

Looking back towards the Rochdale end of Mumps station, 18 December 1968. Whilst work continues beneath the Bridge 24 this view gives us an opportunity to appreciate the distant curvature of the lines approaching the station. On the left-hand side, the wall of the locking room of Mumps No.3 is still part of the scene, forming a safety wall during the re-construction work. There is a gap in the wall beyond the parapet awaiting to be filled with a concrete pilaster before the new, longer steel girder can be put in place. In the background stands the ex-LNWR cotton warehouse and the overhead travelling crane cabin perched high on its traverser. The yard below the gantry is well stocked with railway vans. *BR(LMR)*

(Right - upper) The scene at Mumps on 18 December 1968. New reconstituted stone abutments have been erected up to track level with bare concrete pilasters reaching up to the level of the 1886 wrought iron plate girders. The effect of rebuilding Bridge 24 was to widen the span through which Lees Road would terminate at the roundabout. A distant view of Mumps (the thoroughfare from the junction of Yorkshire Street and Union Street to the bridges) and Bell Street can be seen at the northern end of the causeway. *BR(LMR)*

(Right - centre) After Christmas and New Year holidays it was back to work at Mumps. A scene of organised chaos meets the eye with track lifted and the new steel girders lowered into permanent and temporary positions. The Rochdale bay, bereft of track, accommodates one of Dew's site cabins on this bleak day, 12 February 1969. *BR(LMR)*

(Left - lower) By the 10 February 1969 the rebuilding of Bridge 24 had reached an advanced stage. Under a thin veil of snow, the contractor's site remains what could only be described as a mess. It is interesting to note that the western side of the bridge has a wider span than the eastern side, the two off-set abutments facing each other at an oblique angle. A new road access to the station was provided immediately west of the bridge. Opposite the station forecourt the Corporation provided the only break in the reservation (against Ministry of Transport advice) so that vehicles leaving the station could reach the east-bound carriageway. The road sign reading "ROAD CLOSED" seems to be irrelevant. *BR(LMR)*

Sleepers, fish-plates, bolts (bagged and loose), lengths of rail clutter the tracks out of Mumps pending attention by the P-W gang. The view is towards Rochdale, the railway at this point resuming a straight course after following a left-hand radius out of the station. At this location, the railway is carried on a form of causeway bounded on each side by a stone retaining wall. In the distance (about 3/4 mile) lies Bridge No. 27 which carries Shaw Road through to Royton and Shaw. It is interesting to note that buildings and streets close to the railway are shaped and aligned in deference to it. Several streets in this location have long been stopped up by the course of the railway. This is a common feature in towns and in rural areas where embankments, cuttings, and viaducts stride across the landscape. Brook Street parallels the wall on the right-hand side and provides a thoroughfare between Bottom o' th' Moor and Shaw Road. Date of photograph: 10 March 1959.

BR(LMR)

The subway seen from the corner of Bell Street, looking down slope to Bottom o' th' Moor in the direction of Mumps station. The purpose of the timber section of the wall is to allow access to the track from the road; note that the damaged portion reveals that the wall extended up behind it to the second plank from the base. A street corner gas lamp typifies the post-war reliance by the Corporation on town gas. Natural gas was, in 1959, it its early stages of development and had not replaced town gas. The two cast iron posts outside the subway prevented the passage of four-wheeled vehicles. Stencilled on the wall (extreme left) is an arrow and the direction 200 YDS. Usually, this kind of sign appeared yellow and was prefaced by the words "EWS" - Emergency Water Supply - yet another war-time measure.

BR(LMR)

The subject of the photographer's interest is the subway or underpass which connected Brook Street with Bell Street. The view is taken from the end of Swan Street and looks across Brook Street directly through the subway to Bell Street on the opposite side. The square span of the subway is 8ft (skew span 11ft 6ins). It was originally built of stone with a roof constructed with cast iron plates. The structure was strengthened in 1961 using steel and pre-cast concrete, one of the concrete beams placed immediately beneath the masonry string course. The arch stone work and filling above the latter was presumably ornamental. As a war time measure, whitewash was painted on the corners to assist pedestrians during black-out conditions. Note the oval metal plate to the left of the subway; this is an indication that the walls have been strengthened at some time. *BR(LMR)*

Although Bridge 26 was the focus of interest on 10 March 1959, the view back towards Mumps provides many details. The camera has been moved several paces in the direction of Rochdale, and then turn through half a circle. The balanced bracket signal consisted of a right-hand doll with two arms applying to the Up main line; the single arm applied to the Up Goods line through the station. A fog signalman's shelter hugs the wall close to the bracket signal. It was at this hut that fog men found a place of refuge during thick fogs which bedevilled Oldham in the 1950s and early 1960s. If fog was so thick and the signalman in box No. 3 could not seen his "fog marking point" (a distance of 200 yards) then a fogman was required to place detonators on the lines as audible warning to drivers. To ensure the safety of the fogman a mechanism placed the detonators on the Down line without the necessity of crossing the Up line. A small arm close to the mechanism repeated the disposition of the stop signal on the Down line. Bridge 26 (a subway) is marked by a plate attached to the wall on the track side. The timber section of the wall could be easily removed in the event of major engineering operations.

BR(LMR)

Standing at the eastern end of Holyrood Street bridge, Jim Davenport photographed this scene in June 1957. A Fairburn 4MT (number unknown) draws a Victoria to Rochdale train towards Royton Junction alongside Royton Junction Down Sidings. These sidings had capacity for 112 wagons. The urban backcloth is made up of ranks of terraced houses which follow the lie of the land, with street upon street laid out in a grid-iron pattern. Up hill and down slope the roof-lines follow suit in a characteristic Lowry type townscape.

From the western end of Holyrood Street bridge there is a better overview of the Down Sidings. A report in the *Middleton Albion*, 28 February 1885, refers to work commencing on the widening of the railway and the demolition of a stone bridge. Moving on in time, a contract advertisement for a new Yates Street bridge appeared in the Manchester Guardian on 23 January 1895, a contract which was let to Thomas Wrigley for £7,023. Presumably the Down Sidings were established after 1885 following the widening of the railway at this location. The sidings are passed by a Victoria to Rochdale service hauled by Fowler 2-6-4T **42631** in the late 1950s.

Jim Davenport

ROYTON JUNCTION

An Oldham to Moston Exchange Sidings freight leaves the Down Sidings on 18 June 1955 drawn by a filthy Austerity 8F **90388**. This clear photograph shows the gable end of Hartford Sidings cotton warehouse. This was built in 1885 by the contractor C Brierley for the princely sum of £17,610. The jumble of buildings dominating the elevated ground on the left includes an electricity sub-station, the Albert Mill, Cromford Warehouse, and, a row of terraced houses on Yates Street. *Peter Hutchinson*

There were really two stations at Royton Junction, one serving the Oldham to Rochdale line, and the other the branch to Royton station. Although Royton Junction station on the main line opened its doors to the public on 2 November 1863, the station serving the Branch remained unfinished despite the opening of the line on 21 March 1864. A few days earlier than this (19 March) it was reported in the Oldham Chronicle that *"It is now announced that the railway [the Branch] will be opened for passenger traffic on Monday next. The station at the Royton Junction will not be opened"*. That part of Royton Junction station serving the Branch opened on 1 July 1864 thus completing the twin station fully. The main station in February 1963 consisted of a brick single-storeyed building with a hipped slated roof, measuring overall 73ft in length by 17ft 10ins wide. The was neatly positioned on the Down side of the Oldham to Rochdale line, in effect, sited on the triangular platform which separated the main line from the Branch. This building accommodated a general waiting room, booking office, ticket waiting shed, First class waiting room, and porters' room. Urinals and WCs were located at the front of the building facing away from the platform. The ticket waiting shed was just that; no more that an open area with a door at the front, ticket windows at the side, the open side facing on to the platform. A central pillar about 8ft high held up the roof. The Up side was graced with a small shelter, details of which are not known.

The 25in OS plan for 1881 shows that no changes had taken place since the 1860s. The branch to Royton bore away with double lines from a junction just south of the station. At this point in time the main access to the station was along Station Road: this could be used by passengers on foot and for wheeled vehicles. A footpath also led from Holyrood Street Bridge to the up side of the station. No footbridge was available and it was customary for passengers to have to cross the lines in order to reach another platform. This situation was not unique to Royton, however, being a common feature of most stations in the 1870s and early 1880s until stricter rules forced the railway companies to construct footbridges or subways. The original buildings remained as in their 1863 position with accommodation specifically for branch line passengers.

Siding accommodation in the 1880s was limited to three sidings on the down side, extending from the Shaw Road end of the station to Bridge No. 31, Woodstock Occupation Bridge. Access for road vehicles to the sidings was along Station Road (an unmetalled thoroughfare) which ran parallel to the Branch from Higginshaw Road.

The 1909 OS 25in plan reveals that significant changes had taken place at the junction over a period of thirty years. Siding accommodation had increased on both the west and east sides of the running lines. To the east of the station, nine roads occupied a triangular area of land, access by rail to which was from a trailing connection with the Up Goods line. Those sidings to the west consisted of six roads which trailed back from the Down Goods loop near Woodstock Bridge.

In the interests of public safety, a footbridge had been erected at the junction end of the station with flights of stairs leading up from each of the platforms. The footbridge had been erected as early as 1884/5 and consisted of wrought iron lattice girders and plates supported on cast iron columns. The section of the bridge over the Branch was removed in June 1968.

Reference to MT6 222 at the Public Record Office shows that in June 1901 alterations to the passenger accommodation on the up platform were planned. The new building was to comprise a Waiting Room, Ladies Waiting Room (with ante room), and WC/urinals. The dimensions given indicate that the building was to be 44ft long by 17ft 9ins wide. The Down platform of the Royton Branch possessed a building by 1894, supposed to be identical with the one on the up main line platform.

Royton Junction Sidings by the close of the LYR era in 1923 were at their fullest extent, occupying land on either side of the running lines between Holyrood Street Bridge and Woodstock Bridge. These sidings, however, were never part of a goods station as such. There was no goods warehouse; instead, the sidings (numbering 27 in all) concentrated on the sorting of countless numbers of wagons hauled between Oldham and Rochdale.

It was more usual to find a tank engine at the front of a local stopping train and in this photograph Fairburn **42279** provides yet another example. A previous photograph taken in 1956 shows lower quadrant signals on the bracketed arrangement on the up side near to Yates Street bridge. This was an L&Y original still functioning in the 1950s. I remember being puzzled by seeing another near Moston station where a lower quadrant distant mounted on a tall wooden post stood on the Up side just north of the station. It vanished "overnight" during the mid-1950s and was not replaced. As this photograph shows, by 1957 the L&Y structure had been replaced by BR(LMR) upper quadrant arms. *Jim Davenport*

The Wakes period in June was a busy time on the local railways. The working of trains to and from exotic British locations ensured an interesting procession of trains, and as a young trainspotter I was always full of anticipation on seeing a reporting number attached to front of an engine. Taken on Saturday, 30 June 1956 this photograph shows empty stock returning from Rhyl (Reporting No W658A) and en route for Lightbowne Carriage Sidings, Moston - the long way round. 'Crab' **42703** heads the stock towards Rochdale. Alongside, a row of mineral wagons on the Up side is being shunted back into Royton Junction Up Sidings by a veteran Aspinall 0-6-0. *Peter Hutchinson*

Holyrood Street bridge was a favourite vantage point from which the activities at Royton Junction could be surveyed. Jim Davenport, Peter Hutchinson, and others, were often at this location pointing their cameras in the direction of the station and the tall signal box. The view also embraced the extensive goods yard and the curving lines through the station to Royton. In its heyday Royton Junction was a busy place as the following photographs testify.

(Right - upper) Ex-L&Y "A" class 0-6-0 52427 (L&Y 400), caught on camera in the art of shunting, is about to pass under Holyrood Street bridge, on 18 May 1955. The footplate crew concentrate on the job: their working clothes epitomise steam-age enginemen, who would be no strangers to

daily graft on the open footplate of a 0-6-0, beneath the mean shelter of the cab roof. This particular loco was built at Horwich Works and placed into traffic on 13 April 1901 (four months after Queen Victoria died); it was withdrawn from service in a different world in June 1958.*Graham Whitehead*

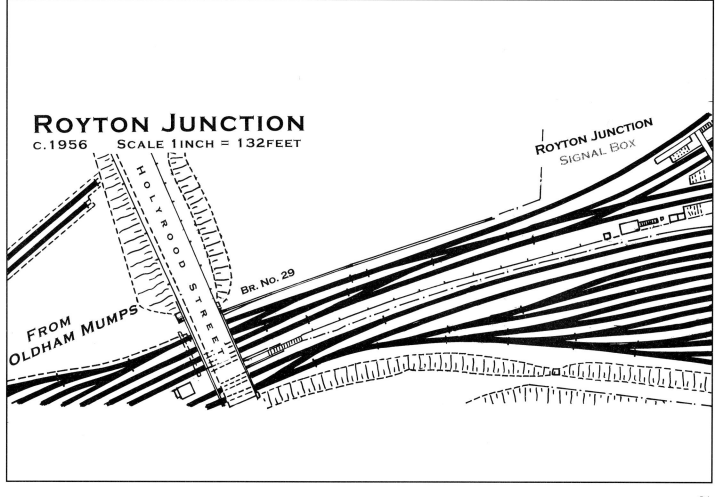

ROYTON JUNCTION
c.1956   SCALE 1 INCH = 132 FEET

HOLYROOD STREET

FROM OLDHAM MUMPS

BR. NO. 29

ROYTON JUNCTION SIGNAL BOX

Now on the Oldham side of the bridge, 52427 is bathed in the May sunshine, in light which picks out a number of features well. Mention has already been made of the cranks on the signal bridge. Here we can see how they convert vertical into horizontal pull, from signal box lever to signal arm. At ground level, partly hidden by a telegraph pole, stands a fogman's hut with wheeled mechanisms close by for activating detonator rods. Note the footboards covering potentially dangerous rods and wires (easily tripped over in the dark), and the yardman leaning heavily on a point lever. The mind's inner ear can hear the squeal and grind of the loco wheels on the bull head rails, and the familiar sound of the wagon buffers clanking irritably as passage is made into the sidings.

Graham Whitehead

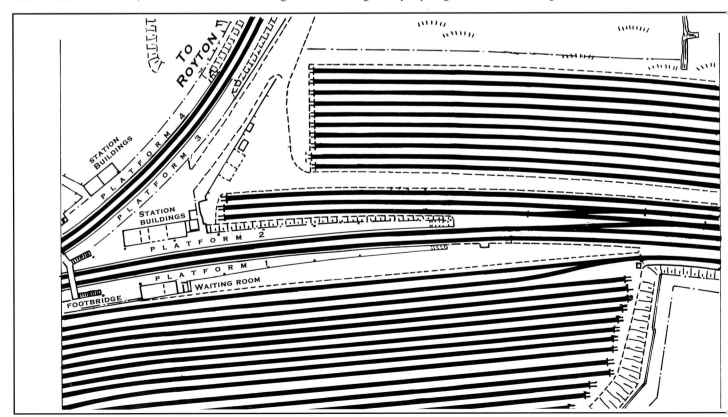

A sunlit afternoon on another day at Royton Junction. The disposition of the wagons in the yard has changed and different locomotives occupy the scene. Centre stage is Fairburn **42288** with a five-coach Rochdale to Victoria service drawing out of the station. On the other side of the sleeper fence, Aspinall 0-6-0 No **52388** approaches a trio of miniature yard signals whilst engaged in shunting duties. Awaiting its turn to leave the sidings is a 7F 0-8-0. The Junction resounds with the sound of steam and to the man on the bridge it would go on forever......   *Jim Davenport*

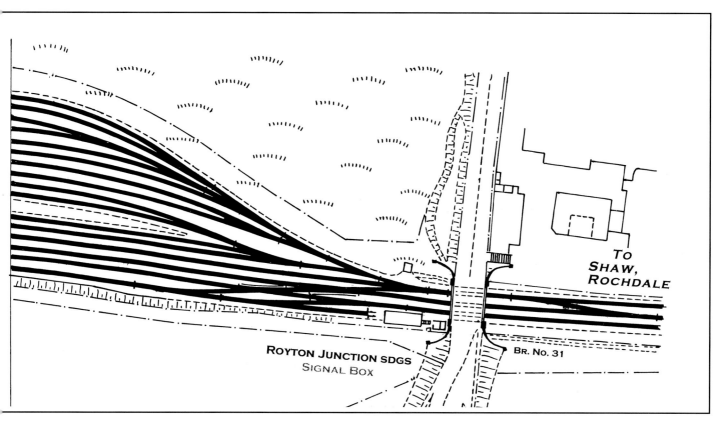

ROYTON JUNCTION SDGS
SIGNAL BOX

BR. No. 31

TO
SHAW,
ROCHDALE

Fowler tank 40014 creates the minimum of smoke as she departs the Junction with a Royton to Victoria stopping train. Trains were scheduled to leave Royton Junction station and arrive at Victoria thirty to thirty two minutes later, and this included stops at nine intermediate stations. The present day journey by 'bus (there is no train service between Royton and Manchester), assuming no hold-ups, takes forty one minutes. Progress? *Jim Davenport*

Local annual holidays generated extra rail traffic in the area, Royton Junction being no exception. On 26 June 1965, a Blackpool to Failsworth Wakes train draws out of the station hauled by 'Black Five' **45246**. There are several differences to behold in this photograph taken seven or eight years after the previous pictures. The goods yard is now depleted of rolling stock and there are signs of natural vegetation springing up between the tracks - always an indication of neglect. Careful observation reveals that the stop and distant signals which controlled exit from the Branch are now LMS upper-quadrant arms whereas in previous photographs ex-L&Y lower-quadrant types prevailed. Far left, behind the water column, there is a coal stage served by a siding. This is a relict L&Y feature which deserved to be photographed for posterity. *Peter Hutchinson*

Royton Junction station on 15 May 1970, eight years before closure. The view encompasses the station footbridge (Bridge 30) with the 37ft span over the Branch removed. (This was dismantled on Sundays, 23 and 30 June 1968). Remaining is the 30ft span over the main line. This wrought iron lattice girder bridge was supported on cast iron columns and was constructed in 1884/5 probably in response to growing demands for public safety. The overhead cross-bracing is a characteristic method of strengthening footbridges adopted by the L&Y and as such, was found elsewhere on the Oldham Loop line: at Rhodes Bank footbridge and at Werneth station. Exit from the Down Main/Up Branch platform (an island platform) could be made via the footbridge, on to the Up platform, and along the fenced path which ran behind the signal box and to Holyrood Street bridge. A long trudge in wet weather. *Tom Wray*

ROYTON JUNCTION

An excellent view of the station building which served both the Down Main line and the Branch Up line platform. The station was built by the contractor P Farrell at a cost of £1,500 and opened simultaneously with the opening of the Oldham to Rochdale line. The single-storey stone building was 73ft in length and 17ft 10ins wide, with a hipped slate roof reaching 18ft 6ins above platform level. Roughly half way along was an open waiting shed (24ft wide), the roof supported midway on a cast iron post. Inside the shed, on the near wall, was a single ticket window communicating with the booking office. Despite its longevity the building is externally immaculate with lintels, window sills, and chamfered stone work picked out in whitewash. The whitener has also been used to decorate the stones around the flower beds. The station opened on 2 November 1863, was renamed Royton on 8 May 1978, and closed on 11 May 1987. *Tom Wray*

(Left) Royton Junction signal box, viewed from the station footbridge in 1956. L&Y box number 219 was in use from 1886, controlling the busy junction and the adjacent goods yard for eighty four years, closing on 5 April 1970. The closure of the Royton Branch in April 1966 meant less work for the 'bobbies' on duty and from their elevated position they would have had a grandstand view of the dismantling of the footbridge. Section C notices for 5 April give a cursory statement indicating that *'the box will be closed, all signal arms taken away, and…all points worked therefrom secured out of use pending removal'*. On the same day the inclined branch to Higginshaw Gas Works was also taken out of use. *Tom Wray*

(Below) Back to 13 April 1955. BR Standard tank **80090** has arrived at the Up Main platform with a train from Shaw. The photograph was taken at 1.25 pm on that spring day. Worthy of mention is the gated entrance to the steps leading from the island platform to the footbridge. The sign over the entrance is pure L&Y. It reads: PASSENGERS MUST NOT CROSS THE LINES BUT BY WAY OF THE BRIDGE. This is the least the public could do bearing in mind the cost incurred by the L&Y for their safety. Turning to the right at the head of the steps led the public to the Branch Down platform from which a public footpath could be taken across the fields to Tay and Holyrood mills. Note that this part of the platform was surfaced with compacted cinders and ash, a flagged surface surrounding only the platform building. The stout wooden signal post is an L&Y original. *Graham Whitehead*

(Right upper) From the safety of the station footpath (bordered by a new wire mesh fence in place of the sleeper fence) Peter Hutchinson caught 48701 on film as she sweeps through the station with an Oldham - bound mineral train comprised of coal hopper wagons. In this October 1966 photograph the demise of the Royton Branch has occurred, and the signal box has only four more years to go. A misty pall hangs over the scene. Is it the mist of Autumn or the gloom of despondency which envelops the station?

(Right - centre) Service 1J71 forms a returning Morecambe to Failsworth Wakes special, on Saturday, 26 June 1965, hauled by a Stanier tank, **42548**, and 'Black Five' **44906**. Both locomotives are in their 'end of steam' condition of grime - laden shabbiness. The position of the head lamps on the pilot engine indicates that it was designated an express train. The Ladies Room end of the Up side building makes an appearance. The main dimensions were 44ft in length by 17ft 9ins in width; it consisted (from the Shaw end) of WC/urinals, Ladies Waiting Room, and General Waiting Room. Alterations to the building to effect improvements are dated 6 June 1901. The presence of an L&Y gas lamp, BR(LMR) station signs, and a home-made plant tub make interesting contrasts.

(Right - lower) The traditional pick-up freight was characterised by an assortment of wagons collected from a number of yards on a round trip. On 16 April 1960, 7F **49618** leaves Royton Junction Sidings with such a freight. The station footpath which led from Holyrood Street to the Up platform formed an excellent observation line from which photographs could be taken of trains entering, leaving, or shunting the yard. The path can be seen bordered by the old fencing which was just at the right height for an adult to look over with a camera. As we have seen in other photographs, lower-quadrant and upper-quadrant signals were worked from the box, in this case controlling the outlet from the yard. Also in 1960, the absence of "orange peel" (the nickname for high visibility clothing coined by footplate crew) is accepted as normal. At least four men are on foot and are wearing dark clothing.

All: *Peter Hutchinson*

Newton Heath based Fowler 7F 0-8-0 49667 was engaged in shunting in the Up Sidings when photographed in June 1955. She was one of one hundred and seventy engines designed by Henry Fowler and was placed into service during 1920/30. Note the unmistakable Midland style tender - a Derby influence. Ransome-Wallis commented that ..... *although they were powerful and economical engines on coal and water, they frequently ran hot and had failures in the motion.* Their foibles caused them to be withdrawn prematurely. I remember these engines working in the local area - never once did they present other than a dirty, work-stained condition.   *Jim Davenport*

From the station footpath we can witness ex-L&Y **52388** (26F Lees shed) moving forward with a rake of assorted wagons out of Royton Junction Up Sidings. The 0-6-0 spent a day at a time shunting somewhere on the system, returning to shed at the end of the shift. The large imposing building which has appeared on several previous photographs is Woodstock Mill built and owned by the Woodstock Spinning Company in 1884. The mill had its own sidings by agreement with the L&Y, dated 16 March 1878. The siding connection was removed on 15 September 1938. This end of the yard had an ex-L&Y yard lamp and miniature lower-quadrant arm mounted on a square section timber post.   *Jim Davenport*

As Fowler LMS 7F 49662 leaves Woodstock Sidings and heads for Shaw, Bridge 31 (Woodstock Occupation bridge) casts a shadow on proceedings. A short distance beyond the three ground signals, the goods line joins the main Down line although a long head-shunt continues several hundred yards to a stop block. The brickwork of the bridge looks as though recent re-pointing has taken place leaving the wrought iron girder in sore need of a coat of paint. Circa mid-1950s.

Graham Whitehead

One late afternoon (4.25 to be precise) on Saturday, 23 March 1961, Eric Bentley could not resist taking this photograph of ex-L&Y **52275**, from the station footpath. Perhaps he took advantage of the clear view of the internal fittings of the cab - and no crew in sight. The loco is shunting wagons into Junction Sidings and presumably the driver and fireman are both peering ahead from the other side of the cab. 52275 was a Horwich product, placed into traffic on 21 January 1895 as No. 422, and withdrawn after long service in October 1962. The lion and wheel on the tender was the first logo adopted by BR following the more obvious BRITISH RAILWAYS which had been evident from 1 January 1948. *Eric Bentley*

A returning Llandudno to Failsworth Wakes special (1C65) approaches Royton Junction, hauled by Ivatt **46449** and 'Black Five' **45298** from the direction of Shaw, on 26 June 1965. Woodstock occupation bridge (No. 31) had a span of 37ft and consisted of wrought iron girders and floor plates resting on brick abutments. This bridge still exists and is virtually out of bounds to public access. Two years departed from the scene in 1965, Royton Junction Sidings signal box was opened in 1894 to control the junction with Woodstock Sidings and the main line. It had occupied a site between the stop block and the bridge wing wall.

Leaking steam but making a determined effort, ex-Midland 3F 0-6-0T **42702** (condensing type) heads for Higginshaw Gas Works with coal train from Oldham, 29 October 1966. The photograph was taken from the confines of the station path and looks towards Holyrood Street bridge. 47202 was a regular at the Junction, often running the Royton Branch for a short distance before taking the single inclined line up to the gas works. Observers relate with glee that with the advent of diesel shunting locos, some found it difficult to top the incline in one go. Steam engines built up steam and rushed the incline; the diesels were restricted to a low speed limit. Steam engines also returned with a long rake of empties down the incline; the diesels did not have the brake power to emulate them.

With his back to the site of the former Royton Junction Sidings signal box, close to Woodstock bridge, the photographer looks across the weed-infested tracks to catch a Werneth to Southport excursion (1Z11) hauled by 'Black Five' **44891**, and piloted by Stanier **42619**, on 5 August 1961. Out of sight is Royton Junction station and the Up Sidings, both hidden by the low grassy bank on the left. Forming the background are the Tay Mills and the low relief of Oldham Edge. A few wooden-bodied wagons occupy Woodstock Sidings. Across the latter, a line of fencing marks the route taken by the Royton Branch within a shallow cutting.   All: *Peter Hutchinson*

Having passed the cameraman, **47202** battles on round the curve and through the station to enter the Royton Branch and thence to the gas works. By October 1966 the Branch had been closed to passenger traffic leaving coal trains in sole possession of the route as far as necessary to reach the gas works. The footbridge spanning the Branch had less than two years to go before it was removed.

Peter Hutchinson

(Right - centre) The trip up to the gas works completed, 47202 returns with a long rake of steel-bodied 16T wagons bound for one of the yards at Royton Junction. The forlorn condition of the Down Branch platform, with its redundant plant tubs, contrasts with rise of new industrial units looming up in the Woodstock area - a sign of things to come.

Peter Hutchinson

'JINTIES'
AT WORK

(Below) "Jinty" 47656 forges through the station on a miserable Saturday, 27 March 1965 on the occasion of the Locomotive Club of Great Britain "Higginshaw Gas" trip. A fall of wet snow did not dampen the spirits of the photographer who took up his position on platform three, the Royton Branch up platform at Royton Junction station. The significance of the trip is not known.

Ian G Holt

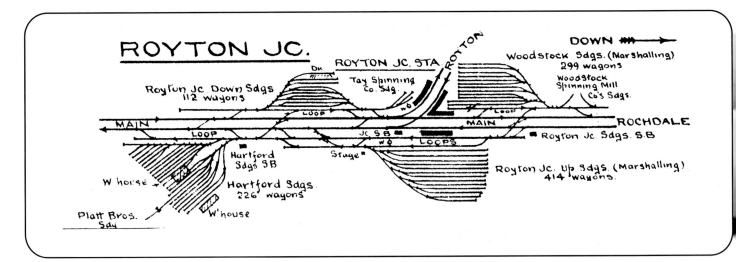

ROYTON JC.

OLDHAM TO ROCHDALE

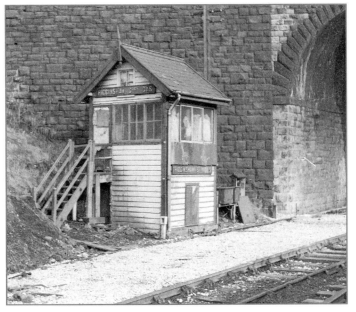

(Above) A scramble down the slope of the cutting has enabled the taking of this photograph of Fairburn **42287** passing under Higginshaw Lane bridge with a Royton-bound train on 13 April 1955. The engine and its train are dwarfed by the stone bridge (No.1 on the Branch) which had a skew span of 32ft. The square span of 26ft was quite narrow but the bridge made up for it by the height of the arch above rail level. This was the point at which the inclined line up to Higginshaw Gas Works began: the beginning of the line can be seen in front of the engine. Part of Higginshaw Sidings Gas signal box sneaks into view on the left, but more about this box in another caption.   *Graham Whitehead*

(Left) The diminutive Higginshaw Sidings Gas signal box stood at the bottom of the cutting next to the Up side flank of Bridge 1. It was opened as LY 248 in 1885 principally to serve the gas works. Measuring 10ft by 10ft by 6ft the box accommodated an RSC 9 lever frame (7w 2s). Working in it must have been a nightmare since there was hardly room to swing a cat. The box was photographed by **Tom Wray** on 15 March 1970, just in the nick of time as it was closed on 6 April following.

THE ROYTON BRANCH

In October 1958 the Royton Branch received attention in the form of track re-laying. Wreathed in steam, an unidentified Austerity has the task of drawing a rake of bogie bolster wagons laden with stacks of rails and sleepers. It is not certain whether the load is being propelled 'bang road' or hauled towards Higginshaw Lane bridge. From the bridge a good view is obtained of the curving branch, first under Salmon bridge (No. 2) and beyond, under Turf Lane bridge (No. 3). The inclined single line was protected in both directions by miniature arm signals - both under the control of Higginshaw box. Note the signal on the Up side of the main line. Not only is it track circuited, but the arm is back by a sight board perched on its own post! Enveloped in industrial smog, a few of Royton's mill chimneys reach for the sky. *Jim Davenport*

The 1¼ miles long Branch left Royton Junction and continued in a series of gentle curves towards the terminal station. The ruling gradient for ½ mile fell at 1 in 62 on the approach to the Station as far as Royton Station signal box. The station consisted of a single platform which was served by the Down line of the Branch; a crossover at the Station allowed trains to leave along the Up line back to the Junction. Station facilities were basic: these consisted of a Ladies Waiting Room, Gents, Store Room, Lamp Room, Porters Room, Station Master's Office, Booking Office and Booking Hall. Public access to the Station could be made from High Barn Street, in the vicinity of the Railway Hotel.

A large 5 - storey brick goods shed flanked the Station and was served by a single siding which ran alongside. From Shaw Road Bridge (No. 4) an interested observer would have seen an array of sidings spreading out on either side of the passenger station. The goods yard had a capacity of 376 wagons; that of the of coal yard on the opposite side, 264 wagons. The goods and coal facilities at Royton closed on 2 November 1964.

On the Up side, adjacent to Bridge No. 4, stood Royton Station signal box. This timber box opened as LY No.247 in 1908 and replaced an earlier box which had been sited 190 yards further east. The box housed an L&Y 60 lever back frame (39 working, 21 spare). It was reduced to ground frame status on 7 April 1966, this closing on 6 July 1968.

Users of Royton Station during the 1950s must have had much to complain about. As early as September 1956 the rehabilitation of the run-down station was under consideration by BR (LMR), especially in view of the advent of DMU services. A survey of the Station had revealed several urgently-needed remedial action in order to make the station safe and modern. The platform roof was described as *"in a bad state of disrepair and in places positively dangerous"*. It was decided to remove eleven of the roof bays and leave nine in position against the platform building. The platform was to be resurfaced whilst the Booking Hall entrance was to be modernised so that it presented a more imposing and inviting face to the public. Even the Gents was to receive attention, as were the dilapidated coal store and lamp room.

As was the usual practice in the 1950s, the station, goods shed, goods yard, coal sidings were illuminated by gas lighting. Only the goods shed was provided with electricity for power utilities. Electric lighting at the station was also recommended.

This extensive rehabilitation was not carried out. Despite the imminent DMU services, it was alleged two years later that *"during high winds, it is common for pieces of glass to fall from the verandah of Royton Station"*. In August 1958, remedial work lay in abeyance and a request for a lick of paint on the signal box arose from a complaint that "the interior is extremely dirty. It was last painted…............ in 1935".

Alas, the much-needed modernisation and remedial measures recommended in 1956 were not to be. In 1961, the station was under a threat of closure, which meant that BR would do very little in the way of improvement but essential maintenance. This was despite that fact that the station was busy. In February 1961, thirty passenger trains and three freight trains ran each way, every day. To compound the inevitable demise of Royton's rail amenity, an accident hit the headlines of the local press in the winter of 1961. It was shortly after 6 a.m. on 8 February that the most serious accident which had ever occurred on the Branch took place. The words of the Board of Trade Inspecting Officer adequately summarised the incident in his report. *"On a fine morning after rain the driver of the 6.5 a.m. Shaw to Royton four coach empty diesel multiple unit train lost control on the steeply falling gradient approaching Royton Station and it collided with the buffer stop at about 40 m.p.h. The buffer stop and stone wall behind it were destroyed and the leading coach, after dropping some 3 feet across it, smashed two houses on the opposite side almost completely destroying them and badly damaging three others".*

The stricken train came to rest 30 yards beyond the buffer stop, the leading coach lying across what had been Nos. 13 and 15 High Barn Street, *"with its front end projecting into their back yards and with some 14 feet of its rear end still across the street"*. The occupants of one of the houses were still abed at the time of the accident, one of the five occupants, a lady of aged 70 years, lived to tell the tale. All five were admitted to hospital suffering from minor injuries or shock.

The driver, who was badly injured in jumping from his cab, was held largely responsible to blame for the accident. To prevent such an occurrence from being repeated, a speed limit of 30 m.p.h. was imposed on trains approaching the Station when passing beneath Turf Lane Bridge.

Photographs taken in 1964 show that the dangerous platform roof had been removed completely; this was probably a BR concession to passenger safety. The end came in May 1968. By this time Royton Station was deemed a *"redundant asset"* by BR, and under Contract No. 16 its demolition was ensured. The Down side building, the platform, and various other pieces of infrastructure were removed. The Branch now closed meant that part of the lattice footbridge at Royton Junction Station which spanned the Branch could be dismantled. The work at Royton Station commenced on 17 June 1968 whilst a portion of the footbridge at the Junction was removed on two Sundays: 23 and 30 June. The Up Branch platform next to the main line was also removed at the same time.

Associated with the Royton Branch was Higginshaw Gas Works. An observer standing on Higginshaw Lane Bridge, with his back to the Hare and Hounds pub, would have seen the single line approach rising from the Down line of the Branch. Below the same bridge, cross-over enabled the short coal trains to gain access to the steeply-graded connecting line which led to the Works.

The Works was opened by Oldham Corporation in 1871. A siding agreement with the L&Y was formed on 3 August 1870 and renewed on 27 October 1876. The delivery of coal was to be by rail from the very beginning, and daily consignments were a common sight in the 1950s. A brief statement in the Oldham Chronicle, 23 June 1956, suggests that after 1945 some coal was brought to the Works by road, a situation lamented by Royton Council which saw the deleterious results of heavy road vehicles pounding through the district. According to the Chronicle, all coal had begun to be delivered by rail as from May 1956.

The rail-borne traffic laboured up the inclined connecting line and was passed over to the Works shunters which sorted out the wagons in the private sidings. The capacity of these sidings totalled 120 wagons. Observers at the scene noticed that the 0-6-0 diesel shunters had great difficulty in drawing the required number of loaded wagons up the line; this was in contrast to steam-operated train loads.

The Works underwent reconstruction in stages between 1933 and 1948. As a producer of town (or coal) gas the Works closed in 1966. It then became a natural gas storage and supply depot until complete closure in 1996.

Former L&Y A Class 52438 draws a rake of BR 'blood and custard' stock towards Royton with the combined Stephenson Locomotive Society/Manchester Locomotive Society *'Old Manchester'* rail tour, on 12 May 1956. The trip began at Liverpool Road station and ran via Oxford Road station, London Road South Junction, Midland Junction, Ashton Branch Sidings, Brewery Sidings, Middleton Junction, the Werneth Incline, Royton Junction, to Royton. Jim Davenport photographed the train at Broadway, Chadderton; at that stage it was double-headed by ex-L&Y radial tank 50647 as far as Royton. Jim then cycled to Royton and caught the train again, minus the pilot. The return journey included Clegg Street station, the Oldham Branch, and the Delph Branch via Greenfield, finally visiting Facit on the Bacup Branch. The trip ended at Oldham Road Goods station, Manchester. Some trip!

Closely associated with Royton Junction and the Branch was the traffic to and from Higginshaw Gas Works. In this view, ex-L&Y saddletank **51447** is caught shunting along the down Branch line. The ascending incline to the gas works can be discerned along the side of the cutting; wooden bodied coal and coke wagons stand in the private siding behind the fence posts. To reach the dizzy heights of the works, 51447 will reverse, cross over to the Up line, and then join the gas works line by crossing back to the Down line. All these movements fell under the control of the small box by the bridge. The photo was taken on 12 May 1955. *Graham Whitehead*

The Permanent-Way Department has taken possession of the Branch in this October 1958 photograph. The only traffic on the move is in the shape of a track re-laying train consisting of three bogie bolster wagons laden with stacks of rail sections. 'Austerity' **90123** is in charge of proceedings and runs on recently laid track which remains un-ballasted. The skyline marks the line of Higginshaw Lane with the Lamb Mill dominating.*Jim Davenport*

Turf Lane bridge provided yet another vantage point from which trains could be photographed. From this bridge, the route into the station was accompanied by Up and Down Loop lines which at the bridge end terminated in lengthy headshunts. Two mineral wagons occupy the Down side headshunt as Stanier **42450** leaves Royton with a train for Manchester Victoria. It must have taken courage to climb the signal ladder to the top of the lattice post to carry out routine maintenance. Less than half way up the post a short left-hand bracket carries a miniature arm for Down Main to Down Loop. The Bee Mill, its engine house, chimney, and lodge form a typical industrial scene found in this area. The mill was built by the BEE Spinning Co. (Royton) Ltd. in 1901 and was still operating when this photo was taken in August 1957.
Jim Davenport

(Left - centre) Big engines at Royton. 'Black Fives' **45114** and **45101** await departure with an excursion train to Southport on 17 April 1965. The dominant feature at the end of the Branch was the run-of-the-mill station but the large cotton warehouse occupying an adjacent site on the south west side of the station. A contract advertisement in the Manchester Guardian for a warehouse appeared on 14 June 1866, and L&Y Company Minutes suggest that alterations were made subsequently: 25 May 1875 - extension to warehouse; 27 June 1875 - additions to warehouse at Royton station. The goods facilities closed on 11 November 1964 leaving the passenger station the sole purpose for the Branch. Royton possessed a goods yard with a capacity of 376 wagons, and a coal yard holding 264 wagons - no small accommodation for a small town. The town end of the Branch fronted on to High Barn Street and terraced houses, looked over by the town hall clock tower upon which we are reminded of the sober dictum TEMPUS FUGIT. *Ian G Holt*

Royton Station signal box (LY 247) opened in 1908 replacing an 1885 box which stood 190 yards west of the new box. The all-timber structure housed a 60 lever L&Y back frame (53w 7s), quite a large box for a small end-of-branch layout. Records in the Public Record Office indicate that the terminus was over-signalled, hence the need for 60 levers. Rationalisation of the signalling some time later kept the 60 levers in the box, of which 39 were working, the rest spare. The box kept a low profile until 28 August 1958 when it drew the attention of the Line Traffic Manager at Manchester. A memorandum referred to the fact that a complaint has been received from the staff in the station box that *the interior is extremely dirty; it was last painted, I understand, in 1935*. The fact that the complaint was noticed stemmed from the anticipated rejuvenation of the station in preparation for diesel services. On 7 April 1966 the box was reduced to ground frame status and closed on 6 July 1968. A week later it was announced that the Up and Down lines between Higginshaw Sidings and Royton Station box have been terminated by buffer stops 150 yards on the Royton Station side of Higginshaw Sidings Signal Box. All equipment between the two points was removed. Date of photograph: February 1957. *Tom Wray*

The Oldham Chronicle, 13 August 1864, reported on the effect that the opening of Royton station had had on the populace, informing all that *The public houses were well-patronised in the evening and towards nine o'clock the railway station became inconveniently crowded by several hundred persons anxious to make their way home,* [to Oldham] *and although additional carriages were attached to the ordinary train, the accommodation was not sufficient for all and an extra train had to be provided later in the evening.* A century later, on 19 April 1964, Royton station takes it all in its stride as Fairburn **42279** awaits departure with the 11 am train to Victoria, its carriages barely filled and therefore a running at a loss. The train and the station are dwarfed by the huge cotton warehouse, being large enough to store the vast quantities of raw cotton and finished goods handled by the town's mills. *H C Casserley*

A stranger in town, basking in spring sunshine, 19 April 1954. The stranger is an ex-Furness Railway 57ft 9ins carriage (M4949) which was constructed at Barrow in 1923 and to be withdrawn in 1956. The station roof in 1954 was far from satisfactory, a result of years of neglect. It was considered to be in a very bad state of disrepair and in places positively dangerous. (BTC Memorandum, dated 10 September 1956) Not only was the roof in a dilapidated condition. Improvements to lighting, public facilities, coal store, lamp room, etc, were under discussion as each was regarded as inadequate on the eve of diesel-run services. *H C Casserley*

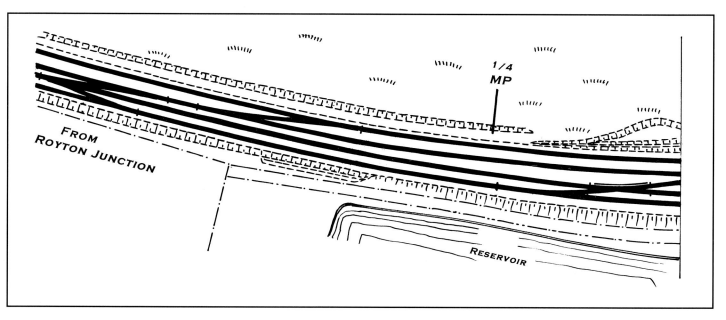

FROM ROYTON JUNCTION

1/4 MP

RESERVOIR

The town end of the early stone warehouse butts up to the massive end wall of the 1892 five-storey edifice. A contract advertisement appeared in the Manchester Guardian on 13 June 1891; it was taken by the Middleton contractor and JP Thomas Wrigley, a well-known contractor for the L&Y Company. Recognition of his contribution to works in the Oldham area came in an obituary in the Middleton Guardian, 2 April 1892: He rebuilt the goods warehouse at Werneth after it had been totally destroyed by fire, and at the time of his death, held the contract for the erection of a large warehouse at Royton, on which his men are at present engaged.

Eric Blakey - LYRS Collection

ROYTON

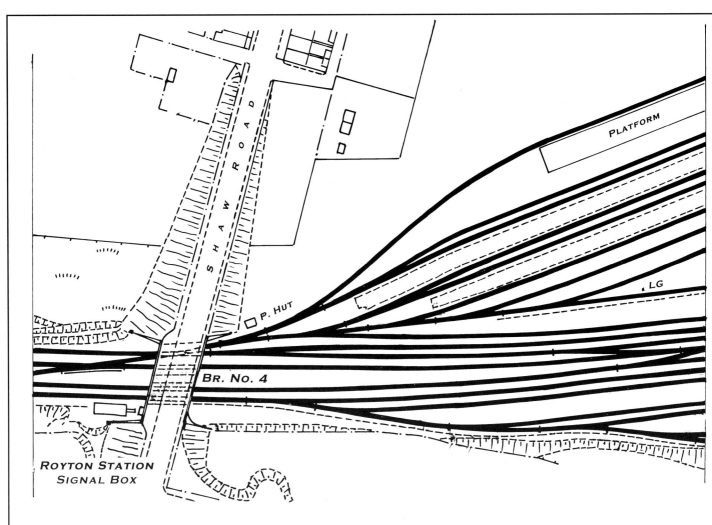

The single platform at Royton on a wet 25 September 1965. The station building is reminiscent of those at Royton Junction, Shaw, New Hey, and Milnrow, which is not surprising since all were to the L&Y standard design and built by the contractor Patrick Farrell. The Royton version was longer than its neighbour and the accommodation arranged differently about the open booking hall. The 490ft long platform was a generous provision at such a small station, more than adequate for local steam-hauled trains, convenient for excursions and Wakes specials, and unnecessarily long for the diesel multiple units. The driver of a Cravens Diesel Multiple Unit (later Class 105) casually leans on the cab side and poses for the camera. The station has been rationalised to its functional minimum, or has it? Could, for instance, on-train ticketing and 'bus shelters achieved the necessary economies to fend off service withdrawal!

Eric Blakey LYRS Collection

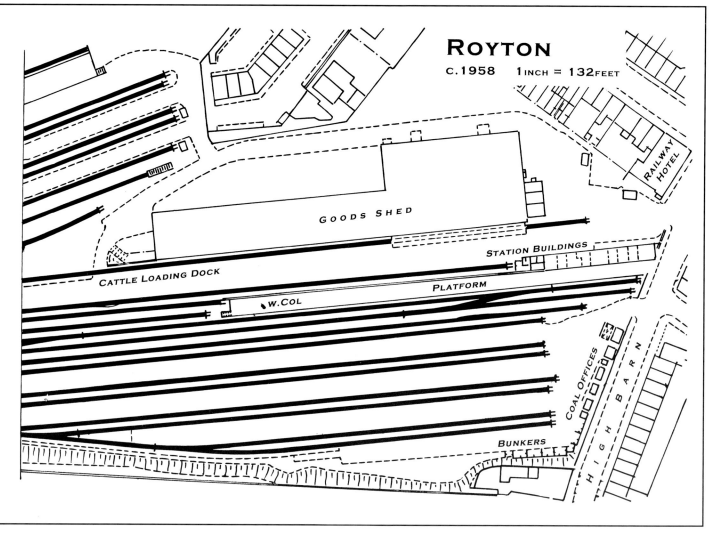

ROYTON
C.1958   1 INCH = 132 FEET

GOODS SHED

CATTLE LOADING DOCK

W. COL

STATION BUILDINGS

PLATFORM

RAILWAY HOTEL

COAL OFFICES

HIGH BARN

BUNKERS

Cravens Motor Brake Second No 51701 looks decidedly out of place at the scene of damage following the collision at Royton on Wednesday, 8 February 1961. Item 10 of the official report into the accident described how the two-coach DMU came to grief by smashing through the buffer stop and crossing High Barn Street, to continue directly across it to hit the houses (Nos. 13 and 15) on its far side at an angle of 20 degrees from the normal, and just clear of the corner it forms with Park Street. The coach punched a hole through Nos. 13 and 15 and through the rear corner of No.11, destroying the whole fabric below the level of the roof….. The effects of the collision can be seen in this press photograph taken on the same day, or on the day after. The mishap was one of the rare occasions that Royton has reached national news coverage.

Oldham Evening Chronicle

A smartened up ex-Midland condensing 3F 47202 (of Higginshaw Gas fame) has brought into Royton the LCGB (Locomotive Club of Great Britain) "Cotton Spinner" trip, held on 16 April 1966. A good view of the large brick cotton warehouse rears up in the background, revealing to us the glazed awning which covered a single siding running alongside. The new style of BR logo, introduced in 1956, (BRITISH RAILWAYS separated by the lion-holding-wheel-over-crown) is displayed on the tank side. The condensing gear enabled this engine to work in the confines of the tunnels in the London area. *Ian G Holt*

'FAREWELL' TO ROYTON

Unlikely partners are 47202 and BR Standard 82003 paired up to take the "Cotton Spinner" trip out of Royton and thereby form the very last passenger train to travel on the Branch. The spring-time day appears to be dank and dismal, a fitting atmosphere to a sad occasion. *Jim Davenport*

THE OLDHAM LOOP - HEYSIDE TO SHAW

The journey by rail from Manchester to Royton Junction passed through unbroken urban areas relieved only by a few glimpses of local open spaces. On reaching Royton Junction the railway reached its highest point, 613ft above sea level, and between the Junction and Shaw, urbanity gave way to a tract of land falling under the name of Heyside. As the following photographs show, although habitation was never far away, hay fields and meadows clothed both sides of the railway, making a contrast with the urban blight and occasional squalor of the previous eight miles. Sandwiched between the Oldham district of Sholver and the eastern periphery of Royton, Heyside remained relatively untouched - a breathing space between Oldham and Shaw. Fortunately, it still is. By standing on Woodstock and Bullcote bridges today, the patient observer would be rewarded with the half-hourly passage of Class 142 Pacers bouncing their way through 'open country'.

High summer at Heyside. From Bullcote Lane bridge Royton lies on the horizon, smothered in anticyclonic smog which obscures the details. The bulk of Woodstock Mill is unmistakable and provides a recognisable landmark through the smoke haze left by Stanier **42557** running on a Victoria to Rochdale service. Behind the third carriage is one of the few level occupation crossings along the route, marked by the track side sign which exhorts pedestrians to STOP, LOOK, AND LISTEN. An August 1957 photograph. *Jim Davenport*

In August 1957 Oldham's notorious Sholver housing estate had not been built. The crown of the hill on the left constituted the Derker area of inter-war housing. Overlooking fields in late summer, Jim Davenport focused his camera on Stanier 2-6-4T **42455** riding easily down to Shaw with a Victoria to Rochdale service. The engineer in 1861-3 constructed the railway along the shallow valley of the river Beal which wanders its way, with man's help, towards Shaw.

Although this line was regularly and frequently paced by tank engines, summer excursions (as we have already seen) brought different classes of motive power. On 9 September 1962 the 10.30 a.m. Hollinwood to Blackpool special (1T69) was hauled by 'Crab' No **42709** and 'Jubilee' No **45661** *Vernon* out of Royton Junction. The route taken by this train beyond Rochdale would have been via Heywood, Bury Knowsley Street, Bolton, and Preston.

Peter Hutchinson

OLDHAM 'WAKES' EXCURSIONS

The return of empty carriage stock at the end of the Oldham Wakes passes under Bullcote Lane bridge and heads towards Shaw, hauled by Stanier tank No **42548** and 'Black Five' **45294**. Passengers were discharged at Oldham from the North Wales honey-pot, Rhyl, before the empty train completed its journey to Lightbowne Sidings, Moston. The Shaw side of Woodstock Mill looms up on the right - an ever-present reminder of the nearness of cotton mills and terraced houses.
Ian G Holt

An undated view taken from Bullcote bridge looking towards Shaw and Bridge 34. The latter was the only structure of its kind between Royton Junction and Shaw, built of stone and consisting of a main span of 26ft, and two side arches spanning 17ft. In charge of the 6.10 p.m. Shaw to Royton Junction trip freight has found a slot between passenger traffic, hauled by veteran ex-L&Y **52248**. Though looking surprisingly well-cared for, 52248 was withdrawn from traffic in March 1962.

Jim Davenport

'Jones' three-arch bridge once again serves as a landmark in this photograph of a heavy excursion train hauled by Jubilee **45710** *Irresistible*, on 10 September 1962. 1T61 formed the 11.24am Shaw to Morecambe day excursion, next stop Royton Junction. According to folklore, the recumbent cows portend rain, although the trippers on board the train can take comfort in that at least two cows are undecided.

Peter Hutchinson

Not far from Bullcote bridge was 'Jones' three-arched bridge (Bridge 34) which gave this view, looking south east. This point was chosen by Peter Hutchinson to photograph a local passenger train from Victoria to Rochdale, hauled by Fairburn **42283**, a regular on this line. A generous provision of carriages were at the disposal of the travelling public in the 1950s, even in the off-peak times of the day. The coaching stock was non-corridor, but the seats were comfortable and the ride smooth. Date: 18 June 1955.
Peter Hutchinson

The following two photographs were taken from Bridge 34, looking in the direction of Shaw. Though not far from Oldham, the scenery has become Pennine in character; a virtual absence of trees and the dispersed settlements add to a sense of remoteness. The location is the same for each photograph, defined by the working distant signal on the up side. Tubular isolated distant signals were considered by A F Bound *(LMS Signal and Telegraph Engineer) to be important markers and as such were painted black ...up to 1 inch above the balancing lever casting...... Then alternate black and white stripes each approximately 2ft side to the post tip. This practice was deemed expensive and was abandoned by W Wood (Bound's successor), in 1946.*

(Right - lower) In June 1957, ex-L&Y 52410 hauls a rake of coal wagons - a typical trip freight from Shaw to Royton Junction. The crew have the time to absorb the surroundings before they arrive at the Junction Up Sidings.
Jim Davenport

This photograph is somewhat out of the ordinary. Patriot 4-6-0 **45517** works tender first with a Bridlington to Oldham return holiday extra, on 24 June 1961. According to *Ian Holt*, who took this photograph, the Patriot made regular appearances at Rochdale, especially on the Liverpool to Newcastle service (it was a Bank Hall engine), but its passage along the line through Heyside was unusual. If the carriages look different, they are. The rake is made up of BR(NE) stock pressed into service during a peak holiday period.

More empty carriage stock heads for Oldham hauled by 'Black Five' **44734**. Bearing the reporting number C724, the train is to form the 11.30am Mumps to Southport excursion and is seen leaving the three-arch bridge on 17 April 1960. The day looks promising with strong Spring sunshine casting dark shadows as well as reflecting on the white ballast. *Peter Hutchinson*

A lineside view of the 11.35am Shaw to Southport excursion (1Z16) soon after leaving Shaw, hauled by 'Black Five' **45076**, on 16 September 1962. Drifting smoke hides the rear end of the train which is passing under Bridge 34. The cultivated fields near the railway contrast with the bare high ground (suitable for livestock grazing) forming Shaw Side, a bold eminence rising to 672ft above sea level. *Peter Hutchinson*

A June 1964 view of the public footbridge now graced with a new reinforced concrete unit and steel panelled parapets, a replacement for the original span in 1963. The abutment remains intact, as does the relieving arch, but new concrete steps and steel railings have been added to ensure public safety. Britannia Class 4-6-0 No **70045** *Lord Rowallan* leaves the station with a Blackpool special at the commencement of the local Wakes. In the opposite direction, a Derby 'Lightweight' DMU (later Class 108) approaches with a Victoria to Rochdale service. *Ian G Holt*

SHAW & CROMPTON

This official view of Shaw station and near environs encompasses almost everything that the railway at the town had to offer. From the 'six-foot' the photographer has framed the station and the imposing goods warehouse within the station footbridge. In the foreground are the timber-surfaced level crossing and its gates, a corner of the signal box, and a portion of the station master's house with a slated roof. Conscious that she is caught on camera, the lady with pram and child gazes in the photographer's direction, while a station employee loiters near the station footbridge stairs in anticipation of the arrival of a DMU on its way to Manchester.   *BR(LMR)*

An edition of Bartholomew's Gazetteer (circa 1961) gives the following abbreviated details of the township of Shaw: *"eccl. district and village., with ry. Sta. (S. and Crompton), LMS. S.E. Lancs; dist., pop.512; vil on r. Beal, 3$\frac{1}{2}$ N. of Oldham; alt. of ry. sta. 575ft."* I remember sitting at the side of Buckstones Road which climbs steeply out of Shaw towards Grains Bar, Oldham, and observing from high the multitude of mill chimneys. In the early 1950s most of these had plumes of smoke drifting from them; the Lancashire cotton industry was then holding its own - just - against foreign competition and the introduction of artificial fibres.

Although so close to neighbouring Oldham, the epitome of the cotton spinning industry, Shaw was a secondary centre of the same with a large number of mills. In 1910, for example, a cluster of 18 mills lay within half a mile of the Shaw station. (This had increased to 20 by 1930). Not everyone worked in the spinning mills, but a large percentage of the employable population did.

Beal Lane ran south eastwards from the town centre and crossed the railway on the level where the River Beal was culverted beneath in a 10ft span brick arch. The LYR located its station on the Rochdale side of the level crossing with ample provision for passenger convenience on the down platform, that side of

the station being nearest the town centre. A contract advertisement for the construction of the station appeared in the Manchester Guardian in August 1862; L&Y Board Minutes, dated 3 September, reveal that the *"Tender of Mr Patrick Farrell, of Ordsall Hill Works, Regent Road, Salford, £4,595, recommended to the Board for acceptance for stations at Milnrow, Shaw, and Royton....."*. Mr Farrell did well out of the Oldham to Rochdale line, also securing the contract for Royton Junction and New Hey stations, and the goods sheds at Milnrow, Shaw, and Royton, estimated in total to cost £5,301. The name of the station, Shaw, prevailed until 1 December 1897, becoming Shaw and Crompton until reverting to Shaw again on 6 May 1974. The original booking office closed in 1969 and the station building demolished in 1973, the bricks finding new use to build new shelters. Refurbishment of the station occurred in September 1990 along with the appendage "Crompton" to the name of the station as a result of parish council pressure.

Confined to an area of land bounded by Beal Lane, Oak Street, and the railway, lay Shaw goods station. Access to this by road was from Beal Lane, on the town centre side of the level crossing, and at the corner of Beal Lane and Oak Street; access by

The public footbridge from the opposite side of the level crossing - and not a soul in sight! As early as 1908 Crompton U D Council complained to the L&Y that the level crossing was a public danger, despite the footbridge ......arising from almost simultaneous arrival and departure of trains in opposite directions at the time when the workpeople are leaving work between 5.30 and 6 o'clock in the evening. The problem was real enough. When the gates were closed to road traffic, hordes of workpeople could not reach the up platform but had to wait in large numbers until they opened. The Council suggested that an overhead landing or stairway between the footbridge and the up platform would solve the problem. The Company would have none of it, its chief traffic manager C W Bayley pointing out that ......*there are two footbridges at the station, and it was not possible to vary the times of trains in question.* In January 1911, a further complaint was made, referring to the bad condition of the level crossing, Beal Lane, and requesting that the same should be put in order. The onset of the Great War ensured that no such work was undertaken. **BR(LMR)**

rail had to be made by back-shunting from a connection with a sid-ing loop on the down side. The yard possessed nine dead-end sidings set in four sets of two with the usual cartways between each pair. A lofty goods shed shown on the 1909 OS 25in plan owes its origin to construction in the 1870s (contract let to Chadwick & Jacques for £4,420, 15 May 1872), and to a later extension undertaken by W A Peters (£12,387), according to Company Minutes dated 13 October 1885. The final building measured 295ft by 50ft and it dominated the area north of the station. The Minutes do not include the rebuilding of the station which it is surmised to have occurred in the 1880s when the L&Y were active in station renewals.

Connected with the goods station was a row of coal mer-chants' offices. These were tucked away in the corner of the yard formed by the junction of Beal Lane and Oak Street. When coal was burned in the mill boilers and in the fires of every home, the merchants ran their businesses in that corner of the yard. An LMS rating plans records their names which readers might well-remember: Hemingway; Ormerod; Crompton Co-op Society; Smith & Gregson; James Fielding & Sons; J E Southern & Co., T K Stott; and J Wright. A cattle loading dock, lying adjacent to Oak Street, was served by two sidings reached from the down line, and a third entrance to the goods facilities faced on to Oak Street where it assumed a sharp bend towards Linney Lane.

A small coal mine had existed to the east of the station, near Grains Road: this was Bank House Colliery which pre-dated the coming of the railway. A long single-line branch curved away from an up loop and crossed the river Beal. It was listed as Wild's Siding in the working timetable for January 1869 and later as Bank House & Wild's Sidings in 1877. Siding agreements between the Oldham, Middleton & Rochdale Coal Co. and the LYR were made in 1888 and 1897. The branch to the colliery was removed in 1902.

The visitor to Shaw today may care to amble down Beal Lane from the town centre and pause awhile at the level crossing. All that remains of that once-busy crossing are low unequal-length platforms (with their bus shelter accommoda-tion), Shaw signal box (showing signs of support using breeze blocks) and the public footbridge designed to keep pedestrians on the move when the electrically controlled barriers are close to road traffic. The footbridge was renovated in the early 1960s with a pre-cast concrete walkway and parapets, but these rest on pure L&Y stone piers and bases for the steps. In place of part of the goods yard there is now a rail users' car park which can be entered from Beal Lane near *"Station House"*.

Beyond the station on the Rochdale side the track has been singled; the former up line now conveys traffic in both direc-

A close-up of the town side of Bridge 39. The view was taken at the Royton Junction end of the up platform and clearly shows the disposition of the stone abutment and the steps leading up to the timber span. Below the L&Y signs there exists a 10ft wide relieving arch, railed of on the road side to prevent the ingress of children and animals. An important requirement are the two smoke deflector plates attached to the underside of the timber span: blasts of hot, sulphurous smoke, charged with burning cinders, were not conducive to the durability of timber. Date: 9 October 1958. *BR(LMR)*

tions. For turn-back trains at Shaw, a short stub of the original down line survives so allowing down trains to clear the cross-over on to the up line. Those trains destined for Rochdale swing off the stub and on to the single line by means of a second cross-over at the Rochdale end.

The route of the railway to the north of Shaw station followed the shallow valley of the river Beal, a stream which, instead of taking its natural course, has been diverted and straightened to comply with the path of the railway. Even the turnpike road between Shaw and Rochdale was forced to assume a distinct kink in its alignment at Jubilee where it crossed over the railway, to continue on to New Hey on the northern side.

The minor industrial complex at Jubilee was based on the presence of a small but productive colliery. Mined from the earliest years of the Nineteenth Century it was, by 1850, (according to a mine inspector's survey) owned by Evans & Barker. Captain Yolland's Ordnance Survey map, published after the opening of the Oldham to Rochdale line, shows the existence of Jubilee Colliery lying immediately to the east of the railway, about one mile north of Shaw station. The LYR working timetable for

January 1869 mentions that there was a siding connection with the colliery and that up trains were not allowed to detach wagons at the siding. Instead, this was to be done by pilot-trips worked from Milnrow and Shaw.

The 1871 edition of Worrall's Directory of Oldham indicates that the colliery was then owned by the Oldham, Middleton and Rochdale Coal Company, and by 1891, the same Directory states that the concern lay in the hands of Platt Bros. Ltd. The demands for coke for this company's furnaces at both works led to a siding agreement with the LYR (No.199), dated 5 December 1896. This agreement allowed the transport of coke by private-owner wagons to the Company's works. The insatiable demand for coking coal was satisfied by Platt's possession of two other collieries: Butterworth Hall, Milnrow, and Moston Colliery, Manchester. The workings at Jubilee involved a shallow shaft of 250ft depth, two banks of coke ovens, an engine house and winding gear, enough to keep about two hundred employees fully occupied by day and night in 1912.

The 25in OS plan for 1909 shows the extent of the colliery and the associated sidings which trailed off an Up Loop line.

109

Mining ceased at Jubilee in 1932 despite the fact that much coal remained underground. Thereafter, Platt Bros. relied heavily for supplies of coke from Moston Colliery many miles away.

One unusual feature of the industrial scene at Shaw was the presence of an aircraft factory. This was opened in 1914 and occupied the newly constructed Lilac Mill which had not been brought into use as a spinning mill. Alterations were made to the mill to furnish headroom, this involving the removal of an entire floor. A single-storey building was added on the Oldham side of the mill, and a pair of sidings connected to the Up main line. The Anglo American Aircraft Company was to manufacture sub-assemblies for the Oldham Aircraft Factory in Chadderton but even before the Lilac Mill had been converted, the Armistice had been signed in November 1918. Despite the aircraft company's ephemeral existence the district council urged the L&Y to put on extra trains for workers at the factory. Council Minutes dated 4 March 1918 reported that *"The Clerk was instructed to write to the Lancashire & Yorkshire Railway Company as to the necessity for improvement in the Railway Service from Shaw between 5.30 and 6.30, in view of the large increase of passengers owing to the commencement of National Aircraft Factory in Shaw"*.

The second unusual feature lay on the northern side of the Shaw station. The firm of A.& A. Crompton & Co. possessed two mills situated on either side of Milnrow Road. Woodend Mill lay closer to the railway and overlooked a siding connection with the Up main line, this connection controlled by Crompton Siding signal box. The siding came out of an agreement with the railway company (No.109), dated 2 July 1891. Nothing unusual in that. What made the siding different was that it was at some date electrified with an overhead supply. A diminutive box-shaped locomotive with windows plied up and down the private siding between the main line and Park Mill on the opposite side of Milnrow Road. A level crossing here had to be negotiated and this was done by one of Crompton's employees waving a red flag and ringing a bell whilst road traffic stood and waited. The locomotive was painted green and picked up current by means of a pantograph mounted on its roof. Crompton's workers referred to the locomotive as *Pharaoh's Chariot*, although a more explicable nickname was "The Green Train". It is thought by one Shaw historian, Geoff Abbott, who remembers it well, that the electrified system continued in daily use until or during the Second World War. *Pharaoh's Chariot* remains still something of an enigma in the story of Crompton's siding.

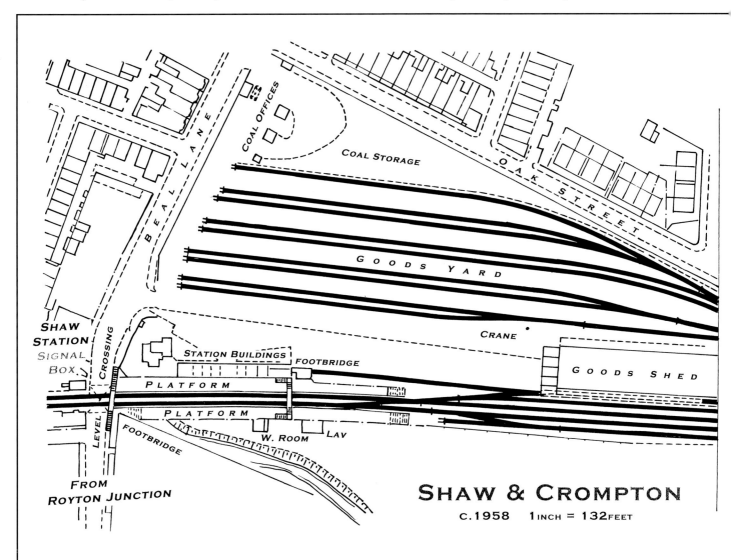

SHAW & CROMPTON
c.1958   1 INCH = 132 FEET

A two-car Derby Lightweight DMU draws into the station on a Rochdale to Victoria service on 25 September 1965. Eric Blakey found the view from the station footbridge an ideal spot to capture remnants of the L&Y buildings which cost £4,294 to build in 1863/4. The station buildings and single platform roof have been well preserved and someone has taken the trouble to paint lamp posts, fence posts, and the roof supports. Compared to the generous facilities on the down side, the up side made do (as it always had) with a box-shaped waiting room. However, nobody in 1965 complained about the inadequacy of the seating arrangements. The size and height of the goods warehouse can be appreciated in this view. *Eric Blakey LYRS*

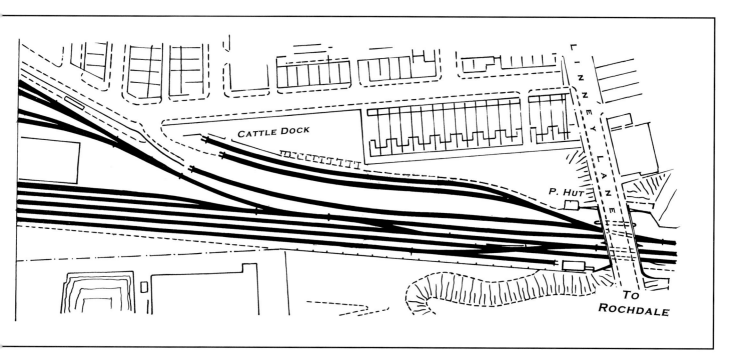

(Left upper) The Up side never possessed a platform roof. During bouts of inclement weather, the waiting public had to seek shelter in the box-shaped structure which at least had a stove. This squat building was considered sufficient by the L&Y - indeed, in 1891, this was all there was. Gentlemen's conveniences were added at a later date. By 1965, the masonry platform wall has been replaced by a pre-cast concrete face with space buttresses. The local bigwigs were persistent in their complaints about the station and other facilities. We have already seen how ineffective the complaints about the footbridge were. Between 1908 and 1922 the railway company was approached by such matters as a very damp cellar at the goods warehouse, who should take responsibility for Linney Lane and Jubilee bridges, an entrance to the goods yard on Oak Street, and the need for electricity for cranes in the goods warehouse.

The neat valance of the platform roof as seen through the relatively modern footbridge, 25 September 1965. The steel-framed bridge (No.40) replaced an L&Y structure which was described by the LMS Bridge Register as consisting of Lattice girders and timber floor. Constructed in 1888. Ten years on, the footbridge steps were renewed, and in 1899 a roof was added. The main station building in 1958 comprised (from the Beal Lane end), Store room, Offices, Booking Office, Booking Hall, Porters Room, Ladies Waiting Room, General Waiting Room, Lamp Room, and detached WC/urinals. All of this was swept away in 1973 and replaced by rough shelters, utilising some of the materials from the original building.   Both: *Eric Blakey LYRS Collection*

An interesting photograph at the Oldham end of the sation showing the signal box, public footbridge, and the level crossing keeper's cottage. The latter structure probably dated back to the opening of the line and was the abode of the man whose responsibility it was to operate the crossing gates and associated signals. In August 1927, Crompton U D Council sought permission from the LMS to demolish the cottage porch which protruded into Beal Lane, and to lay a flagged pavement and kerb. It seems unlikely that the request was refused because the Council offered to pay the total cost. This photograph was taken on 4 August 1968 and shows the cottage intact, and the tail lamp at the end of the "Farewell to Steam" special. And there we must leave Volume One.   *Geoffrey Abbott*

Linney Lane bridge provided Jim Davenport with a convenient vantage point on more than one occasion. In August 1955 his view towards the station included ex-L&Y 0-6-0 **52410** (26E Lees) shunting in Shaw and Crompton goods yard. The station can be seen in the distance but dominating the scene is Lily Mill No.1 (built 1904), one of a pair of cotton mills located on the north east side of the town. The defunct post of loading guage stands near to its replacement, the radius bar standing well above the roof of the brake vans. Shaw goods warehouse casts long shadows across the unmetalled roadway alongside.

Almost twelve months later, in June 1956, Linney Lane bridge once again affords a fine view of a Manchester Victoria to Rochdale train hauled by Stanier 4MT **42653** (26C Bolton). Diesel traction was two years way and steam still ruled the route. An Aspinall 0-6-0 peeps into view just beyond the off signal; no goods yard could do without one of these workhorses in pre-diesel days. Lily Mill Nos.1 and 2 was owned by the Cyril Lord organisation during the 1950s when the cotton industry tried to cling on against foreign competition (which led to imports of cheaper made cotton goods) and the change to man-made fibres. *Jim Davenport*

One and a quarter miles north of Shaw and Crompton station lies Jubilee occupation crossing which served Howarth's finishing mill. This location is one of particular interest to the industrial archaeologist who would also find the remnants of Jubilee Colliery. The small and compact industrial site lay on the Up side of the railway north of Jubilee Inn on Milnrow Road. Jubilee was a favourite spot for photographers who could find vantage points on either side of the railway. The following selection illustrates the variety of traffic on the move at Jubilee in those far-off steam days.

A rare view of Crompton Siding signal box which controlled the entrance to and exit from Crompton's Siding. An agreement between A & A Crompton & Company and the L&Y dates back to 2 July 1891. The textile company's siding was at some time electrified - stanchions supporting the overhead catenary are just visible near the two gates which marked the boundary between L&Y and Crompton's property. The signal box (LY 215) opened in 1892 and ceased functioning on 24 June 1951. It was replaced by a ground frame electrically released from New Hey signal box. The unknown photographer chose his moment carefully, opening the shutter as two goods trains passed each other close the signal box.

John Ryan courtesy Jim Peden

BETWEEN SHAW AND NEW HEY

'Crab' No 42706 (24B Rose Grove) toils up the line from New Hey towards Shaw with a long rake of empty coaches required for an evening excursion from Oldham, 27 May 1961. The occupation crossing lies behind the photographer who has edged his way a short distance along the Down line. The extensively quarried hillside above New Hey forms a backcloth in this early summer scene. *Ian G Holt*

(Above) **With Jubilee House** (a collection of three properties now comprises this dwelling) on the right of the picture, 'Black Five' **44735** (26A Newton Heath) heads for Shaw with a Shaw-Blackpool special (2P60) on 17 June 1960. *Ian G Holt*

(Below) **A sunny winter's day at Jubilee**, 27 January 1962. Stanier 8F **48265** (56D Mirfield) draws a mixed freight train towards Shaw past Jubilee House, over which a cloud of smoke is about to descend, courtesy of BR. *Ian G Holt*

Ex-Midland 0-6-0 43734 hauls a Rochdale to Stoke parcels train past Jubilee on 17 July 1961. On reaching Oldham, the train will probably form a much longer one with vehicles added from the Clegg Street Parcel Concentration Depot.
Ian G Holt

Jubilee Crossing is well illustrated in this 18 August 1963 photo of 'Black Five' **45368** heading for Oldham with empty stock rostered for an excursion from the town. Up to 1932 the sidings of the colliery extended across the ground towards the setted footpath, with connections at either end to both the Up and Down main lines.
Ian G Holt

Facing towards Bridge 48 which carries Milnrow Road over the railway, a Werneth to Blackpool special heads for New Hey close to Jubilee crossing. Bearing the reporting number on its smokebox door is Stanier tank engine **42619** (26A Newton Heath) piloting 'Black Five' **44929** (26B Agecroft), both easing the train down the gradient. Jubilee Cottages on Milnrow Road fit snugly into the hillside, the residents of which have always had an unrestricted view of the railway.

Ian G Holt

Probably the earliest of the Jubilee selection, Jim Davenport's photograph is dated some time in the 1950s from an area of elevated ground on the New Hey side of Jubilee crossing. Class 4F **44022** (26A Newton Heath) pilots an unidentified 'Black Five' on a holiday relief which is heading for New Hey and Milnrow.

B K B Green Collection

With his back to New Hey station, Ian Holt stands on Two Bridges Road to catch this scene of activity as Stanier tank engine **42619** pilots 'Black Five' **44894** (24B Rose Grove) on a Werneth to Millom special on 2 April 1961. The lofty lattice signal post provides good sighting for drivers on the curving approach. Imagine having to climb the ladder to effect maintenance on a windy day! The platelayers' hut has at some time been extended by a single pitch roof lean -to, the hut's postal address being 165!   *Ian G Holt*

From a meadow on the southern side of the railway, an Abergele to Oldham Wakes special passes beneath Two Bridges Road bridge onwards to its destination with 'Black Five' **45031** (6B Mold Jct) in charge. The full extent of the quarried hillside is marked by the deep scars, the shaly sandstone rock once extracted to make bricks and terracotta by the New Hey Brick and Terracotta Company Ltd.   *Ian G Holt*

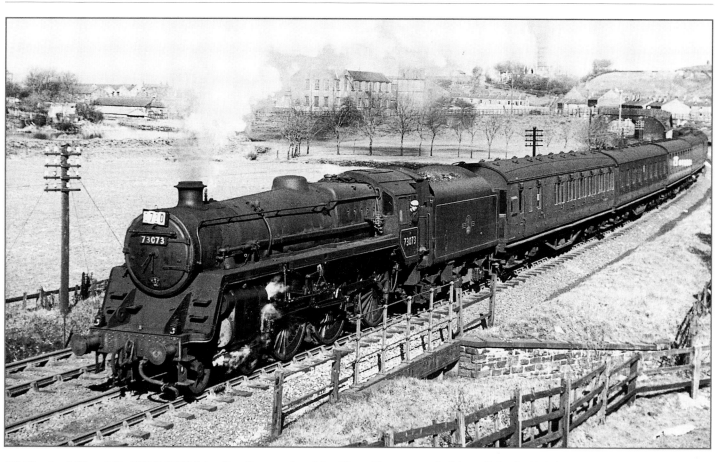

BR Standard Class 5 No 73073 (6J Holyhead) pulls away from New Hey with a summer holiday relief train (C720) en route to Oldham. The locomotive is actually crossing Bridge 50, a minor crossing consisting of steel girders and floor plates resting on masonry abutments. Oldham Corporation water pipes pass beneath the railway at this point and have done so since 1899. In the distance is the arch of Bridge 51, Two Bridges Lane bridge, a favourite place for photographers who could capture trains travelling in either direction. *Jim Davenport*

On a bleak spring day in 1955, BR Standard tank No 80080 (1E Bletchley) leaves Two Bridges Road bridge behind on the final approach to New Hey station with a four-coach train for Rochdale. The sheeted wagons in the east siding suggest that they carry a load which requires protection from the elements. Whether it was an import into New Hey or on its way elsewhere is not known. *C H A Townley*

SPOTLIGHT ON SHAW 1970s & '80s

Welcome to Shaw station, to the side for trains to New Hey, Milnrow, and Rochdale, 12 November 1976. British Rail corporate image abounds - in the station sign, tubular lamp post, concrete fence posts, and not least in the clean cut platform shelters constructed out of the debris of the original buildings. In this last respect, Shaw station of old lives on in the meagre accommodation afforded by BR. *BR(LMR)*

(Centre) On 16 March 1985 the cotton spinning mills serve other purposes and firmly remain part of the scene at Shaw. A 2-car DMU draws into the station alongside the Up platform after previously arriving on the Down side from Manchester. Taken from the footbridge, we look towards Linney Lane bridge, the railway flanked on the east (right of railway) by Lily Mills Nos. 1 and 2, and the river Beal, and on the west by town houses which occupy the former goods yard. Note the crossover which eventually played its part in enabling turn-back DMUs to regain the Up line after arriving at Shaw from Manchester, via Oldham. To return to the city as the 15.30 service, it is necessary for the DMU to move forward onto the headshunt and then turn back via a cross-over, the points of which are still set for this manoeuvre. It is rare for a DMU to find its way into Shaw today having been supplanted by the unpopular Class 142 Pacer units.

(Lower) Rounding the curve a Cravens DMU approaches Shaw station with the 17.02 Rochdale to Victoria service on 27 August 1987. The Rutland Mill survives more or less intact providing a reminder of the days when Shaw hummed with the sound of spinning frames at work. Spreading up the hillside are housing estates which now cover land once occupied by moorland, stone walls, and occasional farmsteads. On the brow of the distant hill the is the ever-present reminder of one of Oldham's overspill estates at Sholver. This panoramic view was taken from Linney Lane bridge.

(Centre & Lower) **Tom Heavyside**